BLACK HOLES

THE WEIRD SCIENCE OF THE MOST MYSTERIOUS OBJECTS IN THE UNIVERSE

SARA LATTA

Twenty-First Century Books / Minneapolis

THIS BOOK IS DEDICATED TO THE NEXT GENERATION
OF SCIENTISTS AND ENGINEERS; TO THE DREAMERS,
THINKERS, TINKERERS, AND CREATORS. YOU STAND
ON THE SHOULDERS OF GIANTS.

Twenty-First Century Books
A division of Lerner Publishing Group, Inc.
241 First Avenue North
Minneapolis, MN 55401 USA

For reading level and more information, look up this title at
www.lernerbooks.com.

Main body text set in Eurostile LT Pro 11/15
Typeface provided by Adobe

Library of Congress Cataloging-in-Publication Data

Names: Latta, Sara L.
Title: Black holes : the weird science of the most mysterious objects in the
    universe / by Sara Latta.
Description: Minneapolis : Twenty-First Century Books, [2017] | Audience:
    Age 13–18. | Audience: Grade 9 to 12. | Includes bibliographical references
    and index.
Identifiers: LCCN 2016038386 (print) | LCCN 2016040852 (ebook) |
    ISBN 9781512415681 (lb : alk. paper) | ISBN 9781512448634 (eb pdf)
Subjects: LCSH: Black holes (Astronomy)—Juvenile literature | Astronomy—
    Juvenile literature.
Classification: LCC QB843.B55 L3945 2017 (print) | LCC QB843.B55
    (ebook) | DDC 523.8/875—dc23

LC record available at https://lccn.loc.gov/2016038386

Manufactured in the United States of America
1-39925-21391-4/13/2017

TABLE OF CONTENTS

1 **WHAT IS A BLACK HOLE?**   5

2 **THE BLACK HOLE AT THE CENTER OF THE MILKY WAY**   37

3 *KABOOM!* **WHEN BLACK HOLES COLLIDE**   55

4 **WHAT'S ON THE (EVENT) HORIZON?**   73

5 **BLACK HOLES JUST WANNA HAVE FUN**   85

GALLERY OF ALL-STAR BLACK HOLES   100

SOURCE NOTES   104

GLOSSARY   108

SELECTED BIBLIOGRAPHY   113

FURTHER INFORMATION   114

INDEX   116

1
WHAT IS A BLACK HOLE?

First things first. Did you know that black holes are made of warped space and warped time? They have mass, but no matter. Their gravitational pull is so great that nothing, not even light, can escape their grasp. They sound simple, until you try to wrap your brain around them. Even Albert Einstein, a physicist whose general theory of relativity (1915) predicted the existence of black holes, refused to believe that they were real. In a 1939 paper, Einstein said, "The essential result of this investigation is a clear understanding as to why the 'Schwarzschild singularities' [as black holes were known at the time] do not exist in physical reality." Or nice idea, pal, but hey, we live in the real world.

To really understand black holes—and maybe to feel smarter than Einstein when you realize they really *do* exist—it helps to take a trip back in time.

All the way back, in fact, to the late seventeenth century. That's when an apple falling from a tree is said to have led English physicist and mathematician Sir Isaac Newton to formulate his law of universal gravitation.

GRAVITY: IT'S NOT JUST A GOOD IDEA, IT'S THE LAW

By the mid-sixteenth century, scientists had discovered that the planets in our universe travel around the sun in an elliptical (oval) pattern. Nobody knew *why* the planets moved that way or what kept them in orbit. Newton

"OH, THAT'S JUST A THEORY!"

In everyday conversation, people tend to use the word *theory* to describe a hunch or guess. "Evolution?" say creationists (people who believe in the biblical explanation for the creation of the universe). "That's just a theory."

In fact, evolution *is* a theory. To scientists, a theory is not a half-baked idea. A theory explains a collection of facts about some aspect of the natural world. It can be tested and used to make predictions. Peter Godfrey-Smith, a philosopher of science at the City University of New York and at the University of Sydney in Australia, compares theories to maps. Just as a map represents an area of land, a theory represents a territory of science. A road map shows highways, rivers, and cities that we know exist. In the same way, a theory is made up of observable facts. A good theory, like a good map, is an accurate depiction of the physical world.

It's important to understand the difference between facts, laws, hypotheses, and theories. When an apple drops from a tree, it falls down, not up. That's a fact. Newton's law of universal gravitation describes the observation that the apple falls down.

tackled that problem in his 1687 book *Philosophiæ Naturalis Principia Mathematica* (Mathematical Principals of Natural Philosophy)—known as the *Principia* for short. In it, he described three laws of motion. Although it took Newton more than five hundred pages to explain his laws, they boil down to three sentences:

- Every object stays in its state of rest or uniform motion in a straight line unless some kind of force acts upon it.

It allows us to calculate all sorts of things about a falling apple: the strength of the gravitational pull between it and Earth, its acceleration as it falls, how long it will take to hit a daydreaming Newton on the head, and so on.

THE HOW AND WHY OF GRAVITY

What Newton's law doesn't tell us is *why* gravity exists or *how* it works. Scientists develop testable hypotheses, or smart guesses, to explain observations. Until the late nineteenth century, scientists believed that gravity was due to what scientists call ether, tiny invisible particles all around us that pushed things down.

But the evidence didn't support that hypothesis, so scientists rejected it.

Einstein proposed that what we perceive as gravity is actually the result of a distortion in the fabric of space and time. Einstein's hypothesis held up through repeated observation and experimentation. So it became a scientific theory: the general theory of relativity. Not only did Einstein's theory explain gravitational attraction, but it also predicted gravitational waves and black holes. Theories may change as scientists make new discoveries. They can be adapted to include that new knowledge.

- The force acting on an object is equal to the mass of that object times its acceleration. In mathematical form, it is expressed like this: $F=ma$, where F is force, m is mass, and a is acceleration.
- For every action, there is an equal and opposite reaction.

Newton used those laws in a thought experiment to try to understand the motion of the planets. It went something like this: What if he were to shoot a cannonball from the top of a very high mountain where, just as in outer space, there is no air resistance? Without a force to act on it, the cannonball would continue in a straight line forever. But, in reality, Newton knew that the cannonball would move forward and eventually drop back to Earth. Newton came up with the idea of gravity to name the downward-pulling force acting upon the cannonball.

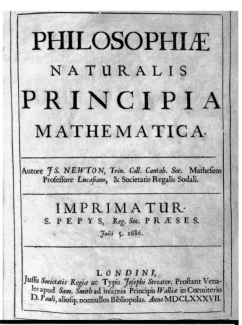

Isaac Newton (1642–1727) was a physicist and mathematician. He laid out what he understood about laws of motion, the behavior of fluids, and gravitation in his book *Philosophiae Naturalis Principia Mathematica.* The book established Newton's reputation as one of the greatest minds of science.

Newton reasoned that the faster the cannonball was moving, the farther forward it would travel before dropping to Earth. If the cannonball were moving fast enough, it would fall into an orbit *around* Earth instead of into it, much as the moon orbits Earth. If it moved *really* fast, it would reach escape velocity, leaving Earth and its orbit altogether.

He realized that the same force—gravity—that pulls an apple to Earth when it falls from a tree could also explain the orbits of the moon around Earth and the planets around the sun. Newton's law of universal gravitation, published as part of the *Principia*, states that the gravitational force between any two objects in the universe is proportional to the product of their masses. The gravitational force is inversely proportional to the square of the distance between the center of each mass. So more massive objects have greater gravitational pull than less massive objects. And that gravitational pull gets weaker with distance.

Fast-forward to 1783, in a village in West Yorkshire, England. The head of the parish in the village, a brilliant clergyman named John Michell, had an unusually keen interest in science. He met with some of the leading scientists of the time, including Benjamin Franklin, and published influential papers about the nature of magnetism, astronomy, and earthquakes. He was trying to figure out a way to measure the mass of distant stars. He concluded that the gravity of some really massive stars might be so great that not even light could escape them. Michell published his calculations in a paper that described a universe with many invisible "dark stars." The only way to detect them, he said, would be to observe their gravitational effects on nearby objects.

THE ELECTROMAGNETIC SPECTRUM

Light, electromagnetic waves, and radiation all refer to the same thing: electromagnetic energy (EM). Electromagnetic energy is created when a charged particle, such as an electron, is accelerated through an electric field. This movement produces oscillating electric and

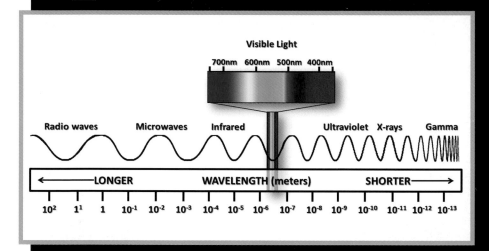

Visible Light

700nm 600nm 500nm 400nm

Radio waves   Microwaves   Infrared   Ultraviolet X-rays   Gamma

←——LONGER   WAVELENGTH (meters)   SHORTER——→

10^2 1^1 1 10^{-1} 10^{-2} 10^{-3} 10^{-4} 10^{-5} 10^{-6} 10^{-7} 10^{-8} 10^{-9} 10^{-10} 10^{-11} 10^{-12} 10^{-13}

This infographic illustrates the range of electromagnetic wavelengths. Longer radio waves are less energetic, while shorter gamma rays are super energetic. Wavelengths in the middle of the range are associated with the light we can see with our eyes. Scientists have developed telescopes that can detect a wide range of wavelengths across the spectrum. They play a key role in observing black holes.

magnetic fields, traveling back and forth at right angles to one another in a packet of energy called a photon. Photons travel in a wavelike pattern at the speed of light. Unlike sound waves, electromagnetic waves can travel through the vacuum of space.

Scientists describe EM according to wavelength, frequency, and energy. The wavelength, measured in meters, is the distance between peaks (tops) of a wave. Frequency is the number of waves that form in a given length of time. One wave, or cycle, per second is called a hertz. Each photon varies in energy, measured in electron volts. We say that a higher energy photon is more energetic. All three characteristics are related:

the shorter the wavelength, the higher the frequency of the waves and the more energetic the photons. The opposite is true too: the longer the wavelength, the lower the frequency of the waves and the less energetic the photons.

This range of wavelengths, frequencies, and energy is known as the electromagnetic spectrum, from radio waves (low energy) to gamma rays (high energy). In between are the wavelengths of the visible spectrum—the light that our eyes can see.

French mathematician and astronomer Pierre-Simon Laplace independently came to the same conclusion just over a decade later. In his 1796 book *Exposition du système du monde* (Explanation of the System of the World), Laplace referred to black holes as black stars, writing, "It is . . . possible that the greatest luminous [light-filled] bodies in the universe are invisible."

You've got to give Michell and Laplace major props for predicting the existence of dark (or black) stars, but they made one critical mistake. They believed, as did Newton, that light was made up of tiny particles called corpuscles. These corpuscles were thought to have mass, and because they had mass, gravity would pull on them. Scientists such as James Clerk Maxwell soon discovered, however, that visible light is actually a form of electromagnetic radiation. Scientists understood that electromagnetic radiation has no mass. As the corpuscle theory of light lost favor, so too did the idea of a dark, black star.

WHAT'S THE MATTER?

As scientists were beginning to understand the nature of light, they were also gaining new insight on matter—the "stuff" that makes up the universe (at least the stuff that we can detect). The concept of the atom had been around since the ancient Greek philosopher Democritus (ca. 460–370 BCE) upended the accepted notion that the universe was made of four elements: earth, air, fire, and water. He described the universe this way: "by convention sweet and by convention bitter, by convention hot, by convention cold, by convention color, but in reality atoms and void." Atoms (from the Greek word *atomos*, meaning "indivisible"), Democritus said, were different sizes and shapes, and they all moved about in a void of nothingness.

Centuries later, English chemist and physicist John Dalton came up with a scientific theory about atoms based on his experiments with gases. In 1803 he proposed that each element—such as hydrogen, carbon, or iron—had its own kind of atom and that these atoms varied in size and mass. He was right, but like Democritus, he believed that atoms were indivisible little spheres of matter.

It wasn't until 1897 that English physicist J. J. Thomson found a particle even smaller that the atom— the electron. Thomson proposed that an atom was actually made of a ball of positively charged matter, studded with negatively charged electrons. It became known as the plum-pudding model, in which the bulk of the atom—the positively charged pudding—was studded with negatively charged electrons.

In a series of ingenious experiments in 1909, Thomson's student, a New Zealander named Ernest Rutherford, showed that at the center of each atom is a small, dense, and positively charged nucleus. He published his results in 1911. In the years that followed, scientists established that the nucleus is actually made of smaller particles—positively charged protons and neutrons, which have no charge. A cloud of negatively charged electrons surrounds the nucleus.

Over time, scientists found even more basic building blocks of matter. In 1964, for example, physicists Murray Gell-Mann and George Zweig proposed that neutrons and electrons are made of even smaller particles. As further proof that physicists have a good sense of humor, they named the particles quarks, after a phrase—"Three quarks for Muster Mark!" —in James Joyce's classic book *Finnegans Wake* (1939).

EINSTEIN ROCKS THE WORLD

In the early twentieth century, a brilliant young German physicist named Albert Einstein rocked the scientific world. He realized that Newtonian physics and Maxwell's theory about the nature of light couldn't both be right. In 1905 the twenty-six-year-old patent office clerk was living in Bern, Switzerland. That year he published his first theory of relativity. Known as the special theory of relativity, this theory overturned Newton's long-accepted ideas about space and time—and eventually led to the renewal of the conversation about the existence of black holes.

Newton had written that the space of the everyday world is made up of three dimensions: east-west, north-south, and up-down. Space, according to Newton, is absolute. In his view, distances never change. For example, the distance from your bedroom to the kitchen is always the same. Newton also believed in the absolute nature of time. He thought that people all experience time in the same way. For example, whether your fifty-minute physics class takes place in a classroom or on a moving train, on Earth or in outer space, it will always last the same fifty minutes.

Einstein's special theory of relativity rejected the concepts of absolute space and absolute time. He said that we live in a four-dimensional world of space-time in which time and distance (space) vary with an observer's

This photo of Albert Einstein (1879–1955) was taken in 1921, the year he was awarded the Nobel Prize in Physics.

frame of reference, or point of view. Your frame of reference is based on where you happen to be and how fast you are moving.

Let's say you're on a cross-country trip on a train going west at 98 feet (30 meters) per second. You and your friend pass the time by playing Ping-Pong in the club car. You're both pretty evenly matched, so the two of you hit the ball back and forth, east to west, at 6.6 feet (2 m) per second each way. That's your frame of reference.

Observers standing by the railroad tracks watching your train speed by have a different frame of reference. If they used a radar gun to clock the speed of your Ping-Pong balls, they would measure the speed of the westbound ball at 105 feet (32 m) per second (98 feet, or 30 m, per second for the train plus 6.6 feet, or 2 m, per second for the ball). They would clock the eastbound Ping-Pong ball at 92 feet (28 m) per second (30 m per second minus 2 m per second). So the speed of the ball depends on the observer.

Let's speed things up a bit. According to Einstein's

theory, the faster an object is moving, the more time will appear to slow down for the object from the perspective of someone who is not moving. Einstein called this phenomenon time dilation. He explained it using two identical twins as examples. Let's say that the twins, who are sixteen years old, wear identical watches. The adventuresome twin travels into space on a rocket traveling near the speed of light (186,000 miles, or 299,338 kilometers, per second) before returning home. His twin, a homebody, decides to stay on Earth. According to the traveling twin's watch, he was gone for two years. He is now eighteen years old. But for the homebody twin, thirty years have passed. He is now forty-six years old!

Each twin has a foot-long hot dog. Because distances grow shorter in relation to motion, the traveling twin's foot-long hot dog would be a little shorter than his Earth-bound twin's foot-long. The only thing that remains constant in space and on Earth, according to Einstein's theory, is the speed of light—and nothing can go faster than light.

If Einstein's theory of relativity was true—and he was quite sure that it was—then he recognized that Newton's law of gravity must be flawed. According to Newton, the force of the gravitational pull between two objects—say, Earth and the sun—depends on the distance separating them. In Newtonian physics, the gravitational effects—regardless of force—would be felt instantly no matter the distance between objects. However, relativity predicts that the distance between objects differs, depending on the observer's frame of reference. This would mean, therefore, that the force of gravity will differ and that the impact of gravity would not be felt at all. Einstein wrote, "If a person falls freely, he will not feel his own weight." So objects in free fall do not feel the effects of gravity, even as they are plummeting toward the ground. In the theory of relativity, the effects of gravity and acceleration are the same. Think about it: Let's say you jumped off a cliff, hopefully with a nice cushion at the bottom. You're in free fall—falling only under the influence of gravity. As you fall, you won't feel your own weight. It will seem as though gravity has disappeared—even though you are accelerating toward Earth at an alarming rate! If you drop a rock midway down, you'll fall together, side by side, as if in space.

This led Einstein to the conclusion that objects in free fall follow the shortest path through space-time. But space-time itself is curved—and the thing that curves space-time is mass. Think of placing a bowling ball in the center of a trampoline. The bowling ball causes the trampoline to sag in the center, just as a massive object in space bends the space-time around it. Then think about placing a Ping-Pong ball on the edge of the same trampoline. The ball will follow the curved path directly down to the bowling ball. In this same way, the motion of everything—from light waves to entire galaxies—is influenced by the curves in space-time.

Einstein concluded that gravity is the warping of the geometry of space-time based on the presence of matter. He published this theory—known as the general theory of relativity—in 1915.

Einstein based the theory entirely on mathematics. He suggested a way of putting it to the test. He knew that the sun has a strong gravitational field. Its mass

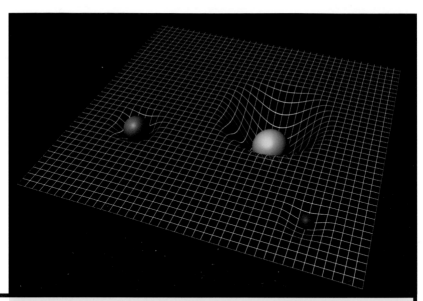

This illustration shows a simplified version of the curvature of space-time. The warping caused by each colored sphere is proportional to its mass. The curvature of space-time influences the motion of massive bodies. As they move, the curvature changes. Gravity describes this relationship between matter and space-time.

(about 1.99×10^{30} kilograms) should not only affect the orbits of its planets but anything nearby. According to relativity, the sun's gravitational field should bend light traveling to Earth from distant stars. Knowing the mass of the sun, scientists should be able to calculate the apparent gravitational pull the sun should have on the path of starlight. The only time scientists would be able to prove the bending effect of light would be during a total solar eclipse, when the moon passes between the sun and Earth. During a solar eclipse, the glare of the sun no longer blocks the view of the stars from Earth.

In 1917 the astronomer Sir Frank Watson Dyson proposed the perfect experiment to test Einstein's theory. He knew that there would be a total solar eclipse in 1919. It would occur just as the sun crossed the bright Hyades star cluster, in the constellation Taurus, in the sky. The light from the stars would have to pass through the sun's gravitational field on its way to Earth. Because of the eclipse, the light would be visible during the day. This would be the big chance to prove the theory.

In May 1919, British astrophysicist Arthur Eddington sailed down to Principe, an island off the western coast of Africa, in time for the solar eclipse. In preparation, he spent January and February observing and photographing the Hyades star cluster at night from Oxford, England. That established his baseline. Then, on May 29, he photographed the same stars during the solar eclipse from his vantage point in Principe. From Earth the light from the stars and the light of the sun were visible. Sure enough, in comparing the photos, Eddington saw that the positions of the stars were different in each image. They

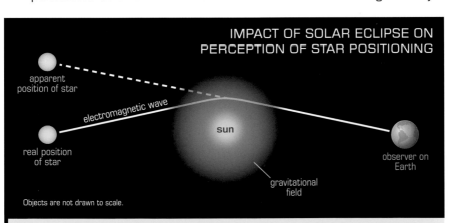

IMPACT OF SOLAR ECLIPSE ON PERCEPTION OF STAR POSITIONING

apparent position of star

electromagnetic wave

real position of star

sun

observer on Earth

gravitational field

Objects are not drawn to scale.

A large mass such as the sun deflects the light of a distant star that passes close by. An observer on Earth perceives the star to be in a different position. The shift is tiny, but it can be measured during a total eclipse of the sun.

appeared to have shifted! What's more, they shifted exactly as Einstein's mathematical theory predicted, based on the mass of the sun. Eddington understood that the stars themselves had not actually shifted. The sun's mass warped the space-time path of their light so that on Earth, the position of the stars seemed to have moved. Einstein was pleased, but not at all surprised. When asked how he would have felt if the eclipse experiment had not confirmed his theory, he replied, "Then I would feel sorry for the good Lord. The theory is correct anyway."

Einstein, for all his cheeky confidence, would nevertheless acknowledge Newton's contribution to physics. In his autobiographical notes, he wrote the following:

> Newton, forgive me; you found the only way which in your age was just about possible for a man with the highest powers of thought and creativity. The concepts, which you created, are guiding our thinking in physics even today, although we now know that they will have to be replaced by others farther removed from the sphere of immediate experience, if we aim at a profounder understanding of relationships.

Einstein was referring to the relationships between the sun and other celestial objects, but he had long been mindful of the relationships among scientists. And he felt it was important to acknowledge the ways in which they construct theories based on the accomplishments of their predecessors.

SCHWARZSCHILD TO THE RESCUE

Not long after Einstein published his general theory of relativity, he received two letters from Karl Schwarzschild, a physicist, mathematician, and astronomer. Born to Jewish parents in Germany, Schwarzschild had served in the German army on the Russian front in World War I (1914–1918). While in the army, he had found the exact solutions to Einstein's field equations for the general theory of relativity. These are a set of ten equations that describe the interaction of gravity as a result of the curvature of space-time by matter and energy. Schwarzschild wrote to Einstein to tell him of the solutions, knowing that Einstein himself had only come up with approximate solutions to the mathematical equations. The equations and their solution describe the space-time surrounding a spherical,

Karl Schwarzschild solved ten mathematical equations that Einstein developed to describe the interaction of gravity as a result of space-time warping by matter and energy. In this undated photo, Schwarzschild works at his desk in Potsdam, Germany.

nonrotating object. The solution is known as the Schwarzschild metric.

From the math, Schwarzschild made some astounding predictions. If a giant star with huge mass could be compressed into a tiny sphere with a radius R (the distance from the center of the sphere to its outer edge, or the Schwarzschild radius), the mass would collapse into a point that mathematicians call a singularity. The singularity—infinitely small, infinitely dense—would create a gravitational field that would curve space-time to the point that nothing could escape—not even light. Space-time would curve infinitely too, and all the rules of physics as we know them would break down. Crazy! Michell and Laplace's dark, black star had returned, at least as a mathematical possibility.

While a black hole itself is a singularity, the Schwarzschild radius describes the ultimate point of no return—the event horizon. Beyond that point, nothing can escape the pull of a black hole. Its escape velocity would have to be greater than the speed of light, which is impossible. And that radius depends on the mass of the black hole. Theoretically, if you wanted to turn Earth into a black hole, you would have to squash its event horizon to the size of a pea. If you could squeeze the sun into about thirty-one football fields, you'd have another black hole.

In the following years, physicists confirmed Schwarzschild's calculations. In 1939, at the University of California, Berkeley, J. Robert Oppenheimer and his graduate student Hartland Snyder wrote a paper that convincingly described the fate of a very massive dying star. They concluded that once nuclear fusion shuts down, gravity would cause the star to collapse to an infinitely dense point. (Nuclear fusion is an atomic reaction that powers stars. As stars age and die, nuclear fusion slows down and eventually stops.) Nothing could escape from a black hole, they wrote, not even light. "The [dying] star . . . tends to close itself off from any communication with a distant observer," they wrote. "Only its gravitational field persists."

It wasn't until 1967 that another physicist, John Archibald Wheeler of Princeton University, gave these collapsing stars a name. The term—*black holes*—captured the imagination of the public. Wheeler also famously said that a black hole has no hair, meaning that it doesn't reveal any information about what's inside. The material properties of any object are unknowable once it falls into a black hole. Wheeler went on to explain, "I was thinking of a room full of bald-pated people who were hard to identify individually because they showed no differences in hair length, style, or color." (Some physicists propose that black holes may have "soft" hair after all. So far, it's an unresolved issue.)

We have no way, Wheeler said, of knowing whether black holes were created from "neutrinos [tiny subatomic particles with almost no mass and with no charge], or electrons and protons, or old grand pianos." All the same, black holes do reveal their mass, how fast they spin, and their charge. These are the three elements that scientists use to determine the existence and description of black holes. (The charge is so small, however, that most physicists ignore it when they are describing a black hole.)

SIGNATURE OF A BLACK HOLE

In 1970 Italian engineers launched an X-ray satellite

telescope into orbit from the African nation of Kenya. Named Uhuru (the Swahili word for "freedom"), the satellite was part of the *Explorer* satellite program of the National Aeronautics and Space Administration (NASA) to detect high-energy X-ray sources in space. Because Earth's atmosphere blocks most X-rays, previous efforts to study astronomical sources of this form of radiation relied on X-ray telescopes launched on rockets. They climbed a few hundred miles above Earth before falling back to the ground. The rocket-based telescopes gave scientists only about five minutes to study X-ray sources before they plunged back to Earth. Scientists were especially interested in a closer look at a strong X-ray source they had already detected in the direction of the constellation Cygnus, or the Swan. (Cygnus is also known as the Northern Cross.) Scientists had dubbed the X-ray source Cygnus X-1. Uhuru would give astronomers a chance to study Cygnus X-1

The satellite Uhuru is shown here during preflight tests at NASA's Goddard Space Flight Center in Maryland. Engineers launched the X-ray telescope from Kenya on December 12, 1970, as part of a large project to explore the universe. It was the first X-ray telescope to be launched for this purpose.

for longer periods of time and in more detail. Uhuru orbited Earth for more than two years, opening a new and much wider window for astronomers to look at the universe.

Uhuru's telescopes soon revealed that the energy from the X-ray photons from Cygnus X-1 flickered in short, rapid bursts, up to one thousand times a second. This was a clue that the source was small. At first, astronomers thought it might be a neutron star, which is a powerful X-ray source. Rapidly rotating neutron stars produce a beam of X-rays that we see as pulses of radiation, much like a sweeping beam of light from a lighthouse. But the pulses of neutron stars are regular—and the flickering from Cygnus X-1 didn't seem to have a pattern.

Soon astronomers realized that they might very well be looking at a black hole—or at least at its signature. In fact, scientists can't really see black holes. They're a bit like tornadoes—you don't actually see the furiously spinning column of air. Instead, you see water droplets, dust, trees, or houses caught up in the funnel. Likewise, astronomers "see" black holes by observing the intense radiation they emit as material falls into them and by observing the motions of nearby stars.

Follow-up studies using radio and optical telescopes showed that Cygnus X-1 was not one but two objects. One was a giant blue star that swung around an invisible partner once every 5.6 days. From the speed of the blue star's orbit, astronomers determined that the mystery partner's mass was at least ten times greater than the sun—and only 55 miles (90 km) in diameter. No neutron star could be that massive and support itself without collapsing.

"STAR-STUFF"

In 1973 the astronomer and author Carl Sagan wrote, "All of the rocky and metallic material we stand on, the iron in our blood, the calcium in our teeth, and the carbon in our genes were produced billions of years ago in the interior of a red giant star. We are made of star-stuff."

So what are stars made of? A star begins its life as a cloud of gas and dust that comes together and collapses under its own gravitational attraction. As the gas and dust collapse, the material in the center heats up. That hot core is called a protostar. As the protostar's gravity pulls in more mass, the core becomes even hotter and denser. When temperatures at the core reach about 15 million kelvin (K), hydrogen atoms in the core begin to fuse (a process known as nuclear fusion), forming helium. (Kelvin is a temperature scale designed with absolute zero as the temperature at which all molecules stop moving. Absolute zero is a hypothetical number, as it is impossible to completely stop all molecular movement.) This is a full-fledged star. Stars continue fusing hydrogen into helium throughout their lives, which can last millions or even billions of years. Throughout the life of the star, radiation and heat at the core prevent the star from collapsing.

Stars at this stage—main sequence stars—vary in size, mass, and brightness. But they are all powered by the conversion of hydrogen to helium, which releases a tremendous amount of energy.

Eventually—in millions or billions of years, depending on the size of the star—the core of the star will run out of hydrogen. Then gravity begins to take over and the inner layers of the star begin to collapse. This again raises the temperature and pressure at the core. But the outer layers expand outward—to as much as one hundred times the star's original size. The star, now a red giant, begins to burn hydrogen in its outer core. When this happens to our sun—in about 6.5 billion years or so—it will engulf Earth and fry it to a crisp.

WHITE DWARFS

Any star up to about seven times the size of the sun is considered a medium-size star and is destined to become a white dwarf. As the core continues to collapse, the heat and pressure cause helium to fuse and create a very dense core of carbon and oxygen nuclei. When the star no longer has enough energy to fuse those nuclei, the star will cool and shrink. The star will end its life as a white dwarf star, about the size of Earth but a million times denser. Over billions of years, it will theoretically cool down to something resembling a lump of coal—a black dwarf. It's theoretical, because the time scientists calculate it would take a white dwarf to reach this state is longer than the current age of the universe, about 13.8 billion years.

NEUTRON STARS AND BLACK HOLES

More massive stars come to a more spectacular ending. The beginning of the end is similar to that of smaller stars, with the outer layers expanding into a red supergiant. The core has so much mass that it has enough energy to continue fusing atoms until the core is filled with iron atoms. Then the core lacks the energy to fuse any more atoms, and it loses the battle against gravity.

The core collapses, becoming even hotter and denser, crushing the iron atoms together. As the positively charged nuclei are squeezed together, the repulsive force between the nuclei causes the whole thing to explode in a massive shock wave. Material from the star spews out in space. The star loses about 75 percent of its mass (this is the star stuff we are made of), but the rest collapses into a core.

If the remaining core is about 1.4 to 3 times the mass of the sun, it will become a neutron star. Neutron stars are not quite massive enough to become black holes, but they're impressive. They are one hundred trillion times denser than Earth. They may have magnetic fields more than ten million times stronger than we have on Earth. Still more massive stars—those that started with more than twenty times the mass of the sun—will collapse into the infinite singularity of a black hole.

This was persuasive evidence of a black hole.

And those mysterious flickering X-ray signals? Astronomers found that the black hole was pulling gas from the giant blue star. The gas wasn't falling straight into the black hole. It was orbiting the black hole's space-time in tighter and tighter spirals, like water circling a drain. As the gas moved closer to the black hole, the temperature of the gas rose tens of millions of degrees. The gas emitted enormous amounts of X-ray energy in pulses. Great clumps of gas broke off and fell into the black hole, never to be seen again.

Scientists had discovered physical proof of their first black hole.

THE BIRTH OF A BLACK HOLE

About 3.6 billion years ago, around the time the first single-celled organisms began to emerge on Earth, a black hole was born one-quarter of the way across the universe, somewhere in the constellation Leo. This particular black hole had once been a huge star, at least thirty to forty times the mass of our sun—and much hotter. Like other stars, this huge star ran on fuel created by the natural fusing of atomic nuclei of hydrogen and helium gases. The fusion formed even heavier elements. The enormous amounts of energy released by these reactions created an outward pressure. That pressure counteracted the inward pull of gravity. At some point, the huge star inevitably began to run out of fuel.

Once the star used up all its fuel, gravity won out. The star began its inevitable collapse to a single point— and it didn't go with a whimper.

As the star collapsed, it sent jets of gaseous material outward at nearly the speed of light. Those jets slammed into still-collapsing incoming gaseous material, creating an enormous shock wave. The jets continued out into space, where they collided with gas the dying star had already released. These interactions created extremely high-energy photons called gamma rays—about thirty-five billion times more energetic than visible light—as well as other frequencies of electromagnetic radiation.

GAMMA RAY BURSTS

Billions of years later, those gamma rays reached Earth and the humans observing the universe. One of those humans was Tom Vestrand, an astrophysicist at the Los Alamos National Laboratory in New Mexico. Vestrand was interested in studying the cosmic explosions that produce black holes and their calling cards—gamma ray bursts (GRBs). "Those gamma ray bursts are intense flashes of light that have energies all the way from radio frequencies . . . to gamma ray energies," Vestrand explained. "And they can last anywhere from a fraction of a second up to a minute."

The Swift X-Ray Telescope took this 0.1-second exposure of GRB 130427A. Gamma ray bursts are the most powerful explosion in the universe. They last seconds or minutes. Astronomers associate GRBs with the death of a star and the birth of a new black hole.

WORMHOLES:
SCIENCE FICTION OR SCIENCE FACT?

Fans of science fiction know that wormholes are tunnels that allow travelers to journey from one point in space and time to another. For example, astronomer Carl Sagan's 1985 book *Contact* (also a 1997 film) featured a wormhole that allowed astronauts to travel to the star system Vega. The Doctor in television's *Doctor Who* travels through a wormhole in his TARDIS spacecraft and time machine to visit different points in space and time. In the 2014 movie *Interstellar*, an astronaut travels through a wormhole to search for habitable planets.

To visualize a wormhole, think of an ant on an apple. The surface of the apple is that ant's entire universe. The top of the apple represents one point in the space-time of that universe. The bottom of the apple represents another point in space-time. If the ant wants to get from the top of the apple to the bottom, it has to walk along its curved surface. But if you were to take an apple corer and remove the apple's core, the ant would have a shortcut— or wormhole—for getting from the top of the apple to the bottom.

WHITE HOLES?

Are wormholes even possible, or are they just convenient ways for science fiction writers to shuttle their characters around in space and time? According to Einstein's theories, they are possible, but not at all likely. In 1916 Austrian physicist Ludwig Flamm was studying Schwarzschild's solution to Einstein's equations, which predicted black holes. Flamm came up with another solution, which predicted the opposite of a black hole. He predicted a white hole. While a black hole draws matter into its event horizon, a white hole spews matter out of its event horizon. Flamm thought that a white hole might be on the other side of a black hole, in a totally different part of the universe—or even in a different universe altogether! In 1935 another physicist, Nathan Rosen, working at Princeton University with Einstein, came up with the same idea. Their idea became known as the Einstein-Rosen bridge.

Some theoretical physicists have proposed that wormholes are entangled black holes. Or maybe radiation given off by one black hole is captured by another black hole. If you were to separate the entangled black holes, you'd find a wormhole linking one to the other.

No matter what, physicists think that wormhole tunnels would only exist fleetingly. Once they formed, they would be so unstable that they would collapse. Not even light could make it through the tunnel. So don't hold your breath about traveling through a wormhole.

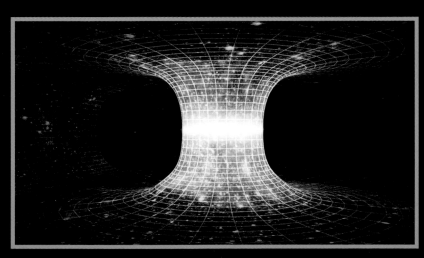

A wormhole, or Einstein-Rosen bridge, is a hypothetical shortcut connecting two separate points in space-time.

Gamma ray bursts can come from any direction. They can also come without any warning. So in 2002, Vestrand and his team designed a network of small robotic telescopes, known as RAPid Telescopes for Optical Response (RAPTOR) telescopes. The RAPTOR telescopes, networked and controlled by a powerful computer, scan the skies for unusual events. When one telescope finds something, the other telescopes swivel to the same spot in the sky in less than three seconds to take digital images of the event. "[RAPTOR] can drive itself, like a Google car," said Vestrand. "It can detect when an important event is happening, and I don't have to stay up all night to see it."

Vestrand's hard work on the telescopes paid off. On April 27, 2013, the RAPTOR telescopes detected a shockingly bright flash of visible light, along with a powerful burst of gamma ray emissions. The initial burst was followed by an afterglow that lasted for nearly a day. GRB 130427A (named for the date it was detected) was one of the biggest and brightest GRBs ever detected and the longest lasting by far.

What's more, the RAPTOR telescopes weren't the only witnesses to GRB 130427A. NASA's satellite X-ray and gamma ray telescopes recorded the same event. One of the really surprising things about GRB 130427A is that its energy is higher than what scientists believed to be possible. What does this mean for how scientists think about electromagnetic radiation, black holes, and the structure of the universe? Does it change their ideas? We don't know yet. That's what makes scientists like Vestrand so excited about researching GRBs.

PROFILE:
TOM VESTRAND

Tom Vestrand's interest in science began one day in junior high school in Livona, Michigan, when the science teacher was absent. The substitute teacher played an old educational film, *The Strange Case of the Cosmic Rays* (1957), directed by Frank Capra. It told the story of fifty years of research into cosmic rays and the nature of the universe, with all the red herrings, dead ends, and clues of a scientific mystery. "The narrator challenged the viewer to get involved in this mystery story and explore the nature of cosmic rays," Vestrand said. "And it said, 'Come back in 50 years, and we'll see how things have progressed.'"

Vestrand was briefly interested in oceanography in high school. "I thought [French explorer] Jacques Cousteau was cool, because he had this TV show, and he went out on adventures and built things like submarines and other stuff," Vestrand said. The message of the Capra film made a deeper impression on young Vestrand. Ten years later, in graduate school at the University of Maryland at College Park, he wrote a PhD dissertation on the role of cosmic rays and objects in galaxies beyond the Milky Way. He was especially focused on objects near supermassive black holes. That paper led him to search for cosmic explosions and ultimately to his current passion: the gamma ray bursts that signal the biggest explosions since the creation of our universe through the big bang.

Tom Vestrand sits next to the RAPTOR-T telescope, which began operating in 2008 to study GRBs.

BILLIONS OF BLACK HOLES

Twenty-first-century astronomers believe that large galaxies likely have hundreds or even thousands of small black holes. The entire universe may have billions. "Small" is relative, of course, when you're looking at galaxies. A small black hole could have mass that is a few times greater than that of our sun. Even more astounding, scientists have come to believe that at the center of most galaxies is a hulking giant of a black hole, perhaps as massive as billions of suns.

Scientists are still not sure how supermassive black holes form, but they have a pretty good hypothesis. About 13.8 billion years ago, our universe was created

Astrophysicist Neil deGrasse Tyson is the director of the Hayden Planetarium in New York City. Among other things, he studies black holes, wormholes, and star formation *(opposite page)*. Check him out on the Internet. He explains black holes in easy-to-understand language in this short video clip at https://www.youtube.com/watch?v=PtA7O3AOCPU.

in a massive explosion of space and time that we call the big bang. Less than one billion years later, giant clouds of superhot gas cooled enough to collapse and become stars. These stars burned out quickly, becoming black holes. Those black holes attracted more matter that formed a new galaxy. Those baby galaxies orbited around one another, sometimes pulling so close they collided. When the galaxies merged, their black holes did too. Astrophysicist Neil deGrasse Tyson, director of the Hayden Planetarium in New York City, says, "There's no other way to say it: galactic cannibalism. . . . It's just that simple: the big galaxies get bigger, the little ones get eaten."

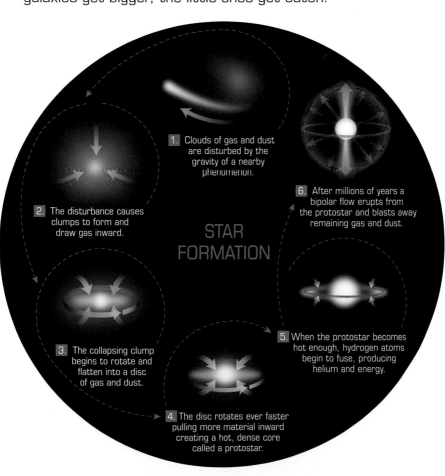

1. Clouds of gas and dust are disturbed by the gravity of a nearby phenomenon.

2. The disturbance causes clumps to form and draw gas inward.

STAR FORMATION

6. After millions of years a bipolar flow erupts from the protostar and blasts away remaining gas and dust.

3. The collapsing clump begins to rotate and flatten into a disc of gas and dust.

5. When the protostar becomes hot enough, hydrogen atoms begin to fuse, producing helium and energy.

4. The disc rotates ever faster pulling more material inward creating a hot, dense core called a protostar.

2

THE BLACK HOLE AT THE CENTER OF THE MILKY WAY

Atop Mauna Kea, a dormant volcano on the island of Hawaii, the atmosphere is clear, calm, and dry for much of the year. There are no nearby mountain ranges to unsettle the atmosphere and few city lights to pollute the night skies. It's an astronomer's paradise.

This is the home of the Keck Observatory's twin 33-foot (10 m) telescopes, each one roughly the size of a tennis court. They are the largest optical and infrared telescopes in the world. And it's the place where Andrea Ghez and her team discovered the black hole at the center of the Milky Way galaxy.

When Ghez arrived at the University of California, Los Angeles, in 1994, she knew she wanted to study black holes. In the mid-1980s, scientists had discovered some galaxies that had very active centers. "I like to call them the prima donnas [leading ladies] of the galaxy world," she said in a TED talk, "because they are kind of show offs."

The center of these galaxies, called active galactic nuclei, is a lot brighter and more energetic than you'd expect if they were simply made of stars. (Unlike the nucleus of a cell, the nucleus of a galaxy is not a precisely defined structure. It is roughly the central 1 percent of the galaxy.) For this reason, astronomers believed that these galaxies had some voracious black holes. Black holes are notoriously sloppy eaters. And when they devour nearby materials, they belch jets of X-ray and radio wave energy.

Scientists like Ghez suspected that most—if not all—galaxies have giant black holes at their center. And many of them seemed to be quiet and not at all greedy. Astronomers had just the candidate for such a black hole at the center of the Milky Way: a mysterious source of radio waves called Sagittarius A* (Sagittarius A-star).

Ghez knew that if Sagittarius A* were indeed a black hole, even a quiet one, it would affect the orbits of nearby stars. Determining the mass of Sagittarius A*—critical to identifying it as a black hole—would be a matter of measuring the speed and radius of any stars orbiting Sagittarius A*. Ghez would use math developed in the early seventeenth century by astronomer Johannes Kepler. The third of his planetary laws

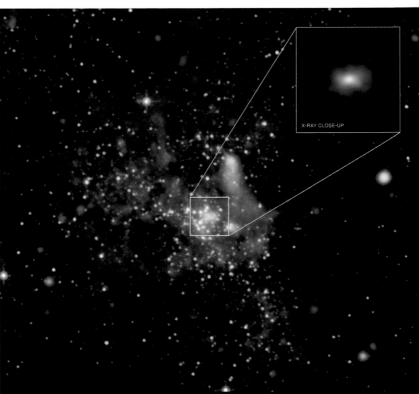

This image shows X-rays (blue) from the Chandra telescope and infrared emission (red and yellow) from the Hubble telescope. The inset shows a closeup of Sagitarrius A* in X-rays only, covering a region half a light-year wide. (A light-year is the distance that light can travel in a vacuum in one year—about 5.9 trillion miles, or 9.5 trillion km.) Andrea Ghez and her team discovered this giant black hole at the center of our Milky Way galaxy.

describes a way to calculate the mass of the sun (or any other massive object) from measuring the orbital period (T) and orbit radius (R) of any orbiting satellite. It's a straightforward calculation: $R^3/T^2=M$. R is the distance from Earth to the sun, about 93 million miles (150 million km). T is in years, and M is the mass of the central massive object (in this case, the black hole).

Ghez knew that Keck telescopes would be powerful enough to allow her to see all the way to the center of our galaxy. But there was one problem. Even though the atmosphere at the summit of Mauna Kea, nearly 14,000 feet (4,267 m) above the surface of Earth, is fairly thin, "it's like looking at a pebble at the bottom of a stream," she explained. "The stream is continuously moving and turbulent, and that makes it very difficult to see the pebble on the bottom of the stream. Very much in the same way, it's very difficult to see astronomical sources, because of the atmosphere that's continuously moving by."

To solve her problem, Ghez used a new technique called adaptive optics to correct for atmospheric distortions. Her technique uses lasers and mirrors in the telescope's optics system to correct for the movement of the atmosphere.

The difference was amazing. Just as eyeglasses help people see things clearly, the new technique helped Ghez see and identify dozens of stars. She patiently tracked the orbits of those stars for sixteen years. She plotted their orbits. She determined their size and speed. One star, SO-2, took only fifteen years to orbit the mysterious dark object! Think about it. It takes our sun and our solar system about two hundred million years to travel around the center of the Milky Way galaxy. Stars closer to the center of the galaxy take five hundred years. The unusually speedy SO-2 is Ghez's favorite star.

Using the data about SO-2's orbit, Ghez calculated that the radius of the dark object it was orbiting (Sagittarius A*) was about the size of our solar system. Crammed into that area was the mass of four million suns. There was only one logical conclusion: Sagittarius A* was an enormous black hole.

Ghez had no aha moment with this discovery. It was the result of decades of painstaking observations. "I wish I had kept a diary," she said, "because it's been such a journey." She had struggled to get funding. Reviewers of her project proposal had initially said, "Your technique won't work, you won't see anything." Ghez proved the naysayers wrong, and that, she says, was pretty thrilling.

Some of Ghez's findings are puzzling, even to her. Scientists know that a star is formed when gravity pulls together a cloud of gas and dust. The increased pressure inside the cloud causes the temperature at the core to rise to about 15 million°K, nuclear fusion begins, and voila! A star is born.

A black hole should be a terrible place for a stellar nursery. You would expect its strong gravity to pull matter away from a developing star. And yet Ghez finds lots of young stars orbiting Sagittarius A*. Scientists also expected to see a lot of older stars clustered around the black hole. They have been around the center of the galaxy for a long time, more than long enough to be pulled toward Sagittarius A*. But Ghez only saw a few. Why? Ghez doesn't know, but she says that working to tease out the solution to the puzzle is "great fun."

G2 FIREWORKS!

And there are many other mysteries. In 2011 astronomers at the Max Planck Institute for Extraterrestrial Physics in Garching, Germany, discovered a strange object.

PATROLLING THE COSMIC HIGHWAY, OR HOW TO CATCH A SPEEDING GALAXY

How do astronomers measure the speed of distant objects such as stars and galaxies? After all, they're light-years away! (Astronomical distances are so great that astronomers speak of them not in miles or kilometers but in light-years. A light-year is the distance that light can travel in a vacuum in one year—about 5.9 trillion miles, or 9.5 trillion km).

To measure speed, astronomers rely on the Doppler shift. Depending on a star's characteristics, including what it's made of and its temperature, it will radiate light from a certain part of the electromagnetic spectrum. For example, the coolest stars in the universe, red dwarf stars, emit light at the red end of the visible spectrum. The hottest stars in the universe emit light at the blue end of the visible spectrum. The brightest visible star in our night sky is Sirius, a hot blue-white star. We can measure the temperature and chemical composition of Sirius and predict that it should radiate its light at a certain wavelength.

If Sirius were to suddenly begin racing toward Earth (it won't), the wavelengths would become even shorter and they would increase in frequency. The star would appear even bluer than it is now. Astronomers would say that the star had blue-shifted, and they could use that information to calculate how fast the star is speeding toward us. If Sirius began moving just as speedily away

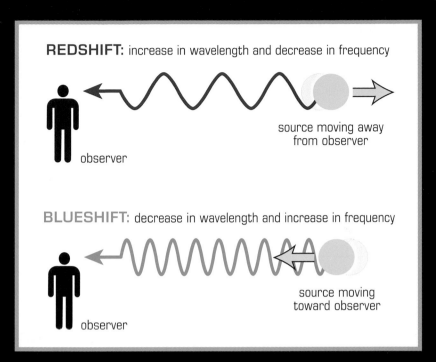

REDSHIFT: increase in wavelength and decrease in frequency

source moving away
from observer

observer

BLUESHIFT: decrease in wavelength and increase in frequency

source moving
toward observer

observer

Astronomers can determine the speed and direction of a moving body by observing changes in the length and frequency of the wavelengths of that object. This infographic illustrates the changes associated with red-shifting (moving away from the observer) and blue-shifting (moving toward the observer).

from us, the wavelengths that reach us from the star would lengthen and shift toward the cooler, red end of the spectrum. Astronomers would say that Sirius had red-shifted, and they could use that information to calculate how rapidly the star is receding. Blue- and red-shifting terminology comes from light in the visible spectrum. Astronomers use the terms, however, to describe a shifting in any part of the electromagnetic spectrum. If an object emitting gamma rays is moving away from us, for example, its wavelength might be stretched out into the X-ray part of the spectrum.

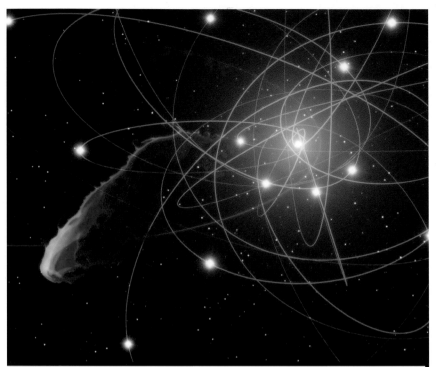

This view shows a simulation of how the gas cloud G2 approaching Sagitarrius A* may one day break apart. G2's orbit is shown in red. The remains of the gas cloud are in red and yellow. The stars orbiting the black hole are shown with blue lines to mark their orbits.

It appeared to be a cloud of gas, with a mass roughly three times that of Earth, in a wild orbit around Sagittarius A*. The object, dubbed G2, seemed to be making a beeline for the black hole, only to whip around it and shoot straight back into orbit again. Astronomers expected to see fireworks as G2 eventually met its end in the black hole.

But G2 is still going strong. In 2014 Ghez and her team observed G2 continuing on its merry way around Sagittarius A*. The exact nature of G2 is still unclear.

PROFILE:
ANDREA GHEZ

When Andrea Ghez was a little girl in Chicago, Illinois, she dreamed of becoming a ballerina. Yet Ghez says she was meant to be a scientist. When she was four years old, she was fascinated by NASA's 1969 *Apollo* moon landing, the first time humans had ever stepped onto the lunar surface. She told her mother that she wanted to become NASA's first female astronaut. Physicist Marie Curie and pilot Amelia Earhart captured her imagination too, and in school, she excelled in math and science. "The idea of the universe kept me up at night," she said.

She spent summers working on telescopes in Arizona and in the South American nation of Chile. She was hooked.

In 1987 Ghez started graduate school at the California Institute of Technology in Pasadena. She wanted to study black holes, but the techniques for studying them were not very advanced. She ended up studying the birth of stars instead and became very skilled at producing images of stars from computer data. This skill was later key to her work on black holes.

In 1992 Ghez received her PhD in astronomy. Two years later, she joined the faculty at the University of California, Los Angeles, where she specializes in black holes. Ghez has received many awards, including a MacArthur Fellowship—often called a genius grant. She is sometimes referred to as a stargazing detective!

Andrea Ghez is an astrophysicist at the University of California, Los Angeles. She has always loved puzzles—jigsaw puzzles, crossword puzzles, sudoku, and Kenken. She says that's why she loves science. It's another type of puzzle.

But Ghez does not believe it's a gas cloud. If it were, it would have been torn apart by the black hole. In a press release, Ghez confirmed, "G2 was basically unaffected by the black hole. There were no fireworks." Instead, Ghez thinks that G2 is probably a star that was created when the black hole's gravity drove two binary stars (two stars that revolve around each other) to merge into one.

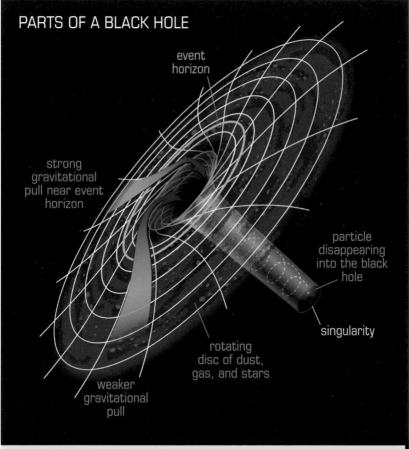

PARTS OF A BLACK HOLE

event horizon

strong gravitational pull near event horizon

particle disappearing into the black hole

singularity

rotating disc of dust, gas, and stars

weaker gravitational pull

This diagram shows how things could hypothetically disappear into a black hole.

OOPS, YOU GOT TOO CLOSE TO A BLACK HOLE. NOW WHAT?

In the 2014 movie *Interstellar*, Earth is an ecological disaster. Former NASA astronaut Cooper (played by Matthew McConaughey) leads a mission to search for another habitable planet. He enters a black hole named Gargantuan and . . . no spoilers here!

Kip Thorne is a theoretical astrophysicist at the California Institute of Technology. He is an expert on black holes and was the script adviser and executive producer on the film. So the major plot points are based on real—or at least imaginable—science.

What *would* happen if you fell into a black hole? Believe it or not, scientists have been playing this what-if game for decades. It's not just a party game. The answer depends upon our understanding of the laws of physics as they work in black holes.

Let's say you are the captain of a crew of astronauts in a spaceship nearing a stellar black hole—ten to one hundred times the mass of our sun. Your ace first mate puts your spacecraft into orbit a safe distance from the black hole's event horizon: the point of no return. It appears as a sharply defined, pure black disk. It is surrounded by light from nearby stars, but the black hole's gravity has distorted the light so that it appears as a distorted smear.

You, being a brave astronaut, want to get a closer look at the event horizon. So you suit up in your space suit and climb into a small space capsule and slow your orbit. The black hole's gravity pulls you in closer to the event horizon. Your bravery turns to foolhardiness when you decide to take a little space walk. You're too close—

you find yourself falling into the black hole, feetfirst! (Forget for a moment that you are being bombarded by a deadly shower of X-rays and gamma rays. They are the least of your worries!) As you get closer to the black hole, its gravitational pull grows enormously. You don't feel it because, being in free fall, you're weightless. But you'll feel something soon enough. As you near the event horizon, the force of gravity is much stronger at your feet than at your head, so they accelerate faster. Scientists call this difference in gravity the tidal force— exactly like the moon's pull of gravity that produces tides here on Earth.

As the black hole's gravity continues its pull, your body becomes stretched out. You eventually snap into two pieces. Soon you are a mess of molecules and atoms, squeezed through the fabric of space and time into nothingness at the center of the black hole. Scientists call this process, no kidding, "spaghettification."

As your crew watches your demise in horror, they observe something very odd. The closer you get to the event horizon, the more you appear to move in slow motion. The light coming from you takes on a redder and redder hue. The wavelengths get longer until the crew needs a radio telescope to see you. When you reach the event horizon, the black hole has warped the space-time fabric so much that to outside observers, time crawls to a near halt. If your crew were patient (and long-lived) enough, they would eventually see your image just fade away.

Conventional theories say that you'd continue falling—for hours, maybe—until the last second before you

Professor Stephen Hawking attends a screening of the 2013 documentary *Hawking*. The film uses his own words and interviews with people who know him well to tell the life story of this iconic physicist.

reached the singularity. Only then would you become crushed into the singularity.

HAWKING RADIATION

Recent theories have proposed that you might not actually disappear completely. These theories can be traced back to English cosmologist Stephen Hawking, of the University of Cambridge. In the mid-1970s, he tried to reconcile the general theory of relativity, which describes the universe on a large scale, and quantum mechanics, which explains the behavior of the universe on a very small scale. Experiments have confirmed predictions made by both theories, but in their current forms, they cannot both be right.

QUANTUM THEORY

Quantum theory is the science of understanding the behavior of very small things such as atoms and subatomic particles, which are even smaller than atoms. Danish physicist Niels Bohr was one of the pioneers of quantum theory. He won a Nobel Prize in 1922 for his groundbreaking theories. Quantum theory is mind-boggling. In fact, Bohr himself once said, "Anyone who is not shocked by quantum theory has not understood it."

Quantum theory is based on some radical principles:

- Both energy and matter are made of individual units, or quanta. (The word comes from the Latin *quantum*, "a share or portion of something.")
- On a large scale, energy and matter behave as waves. But on the atomic and subatomic level, energy and matter may behave either as particles or as waves. This theory is known as the wave-particle duality.
- It is impossible to accurately measure both the position and the momentum of a particle at the same moment in time.
- Any measuring device will affect the behavior of subatomic particles. So quantum mechanics can only help determine the *probability* of the location or momentum of subatomic particles. This is known as the uncertainty principle.

ENTANGLEMENT

Quantum theory makes some pretty wild predictions. Matter can be in more than one place or state at a time. An electron, for example, can be in two places at once, or it can simultaneously spin in opposite directions. It is only by measuring an object that it is forced into a well-defined place or state. According to quantum theory, it is possible that we live in a multiverse, a universe with many parallel worlds. Things can disappear and reappear somewhere else.

The theory even predicts that when two particles interact, they become entangled. Two entangled electrons, for example, will always have opposite spins. One will spin in a clockwise direction and the other will spin counterclockwise, for a net spin of zero. But in the tiny quantum world, particles such as electrons do not have a defined spin until they are measured. Once a scientist measures the spin of one electron, the spin of its entangled partner immediately takes the opposite spin, even if they are physically separated. Einstein was skeptical of much of quantum theory, calling it "spooky action at a distance."

In 2015 scientists at Delft University of Technology in the Netherlands proved quantum entanglement. They trapped two electrons inside two diamonds—one per diamond—in different labs on the Delft campus, 0.8 miles (1.3 km) apart. They zapped each electron with a laser beam to entangle each with a photon. They sent those photons down an optical fiber to a third location, leaving the electrons behind. If the two photons arrived at precisely

the same time (and they did), they would interact with each other and become entangled—and entangle their distant electron buddies as well. And whenever the scientists measured the spin of one electron in its diamond, the one across campus instantly took on the opposite spin. The two electrons were truly entangled.

Dutch physicist Paul Ehrenfest took this photo of Niels Bohr (right) and Albert Einstein (left) at the 1930 Solvay Conference on physics in Brussels, Belgium. The famous conference is still held every year.

The general theory of relativity says that when stuff falls into a black hole, everything about its existence is erased—gone forever, just like that. But quantum mechanics tells us that information can never be lost. According to this theory, if you were able to reach into a black hole, you should be able to reconstruct what fell in. So which theory is right?

In the mid-1970s, Hawking predicted that based on quantum mechanics, black holes would leak particles and radiation. Over billions of years, they would eventually evaporate, or dry up. The Hawking radiation, as the evaporation is known, would be completely random. It wouldn't carry any information at all about the stuff inside the black hole. Hawking's predictions started a decades-long "black hole information problem." Is information lost or not?

A WAY OUT

In 2012 a team of scientists from the University of California, Santa Barbara, suggested a possible answer. They proposed that an energetic "firewall" exists just inside a black hole's event horizon. It would fry any entering astronaut or star to a crisp immediately. But based on the theory of quantum entanglement—which says that two particles separated by a great distance can still communicate with each other—there is another possibility. There could be two versions of the astronaut or star: one inside the event horizon of the black hole, incinerated, and another, whole, outside the event horizon.

Hawking and two colleagues at the University of Cambridge and Harvard University have come up with what may be at least a partial solution to the problem they first identified in the 1970s. In 2016 they wrote a paper "Soft Hair on Black Holes." The paper suggests that very low or even zero-energy quantum particles (soft hair) sit on the edge of the black hole. These hairs capture and store information from the particles falling into the black hole. Hawking told the *New York Times*, "If you feel you are trapped in a black hole, don't give up. There is a way out."

According to Hawking, the soft hairs would store whatever fell into the black hole as something like a holographic image (a 3-D representation of a two-dimensional image). The image would remain at the event horizon in a coded form.

This ongoing discussion among physicists won't be resolved anytime soon. Meanwhile, it's probably best to steer clear of black holes.

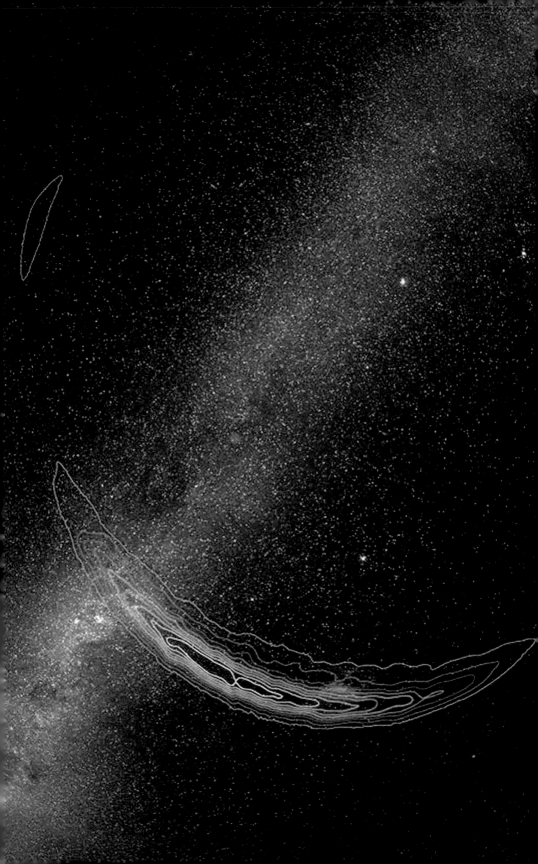

3

KABOOM! WHEN BLACK HOLES COLLIDE

Scientific breakthroughs don't always come when you expect them. In the case of Vicky Kalogera, an astrophysicist at Northwestern University in Evanston, Illinois, the news came on September 14, 2015, when she was getting dinner on the table for her family. Her busy day hadn't allowed her to pay much attention to the flurry of e-mails from her colleagues on the Laser Interferometer Gravitational-Wave Observatory (LIGO) project. This project to find and observe gravitational waves in space is funded by the US National Science Foundation (NSF).

Two instruments operating in unison—one in Louisiana and the other in Washington—offer astronomers a whole new way of studying the universe. Unlike astronomical telescopes, LIGO cannot detect electromagnetic radiation at any wavelength or frequency. Instead, it "feels" invisible gravitational waves. Decades in the making, LIGO had just begun collecting data when the detectors hit the jackpot.

That fall day, a text message from one of Kalogera's graduate students spelled it out: "Have you been keeping up with LIGO emails today? Loud trigger!" That's when she knew something big had happened.

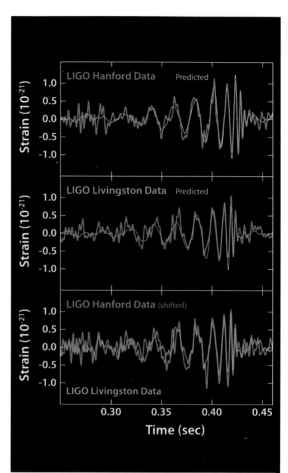

These plots show the signals of gravitational waves detected by the twin LIGO observatories at Livingston, Louisiana, and Hanford, Washington. The signals came from two merging black holes, each about thirty times the mass of the sun, lying 1.3 billion light-years away. These waveforms show what two merging black holes should look like according to the equations of Albert Einstein's general theory of relativity. The LIGO data very closely match Einstein's predictions.

That "something big" was a signal from outer space, picked up by the LIGO detectors. It confirmed the existence of gravitational waves, predicted by Einstein a century ago. Kalogera, along with one thousand other scientists and engineers, had been working toward this moment for nearly two decades.

Kalogera and the other members of the LIGO team—more than one thousand scientists from ninety different institutions—were sworn to secrecy until the data could be thoroughly analyzed to make sure the signal was real. It was.

On February 11, 2016, LIGO laboratory executive director David Reitze held a press conference. "Ladies and gentlemen, we have detected gravitational waves. We did it. I am so pleased to be able to tell you that. . . . These gravitational waves were produced by two colliding black holes that came together, merged to form a single black hole about 1.3 billion years ago."

The announcement stunned the scientific community. Even US president Barack Obama tweeted: "Einstein was right! Congrats to @NSF and @LIGO on detecting gravitational waves—a huge breakthrough in how we understand the universe."

Why was the discovery so exciting? Remember that Einstein's general theory of relativity states that space and time curve in the presence of mass. This curvature is responsible for the effect we call gravity. When two objects interact with each other, they stretch and squeeze space-time. If those two objects are not very massive, like a couple of pool balls or you and your friend, the effect is so small as to be unnoticeable.

PROFILE:
VICKY KALOGERA

Vicky (Vassiliki) Kalogera was born and raised in a small town in Greece, where young people, especially young women, were not generally expected to study math and science. But her parents encouraged her to work hard and pursue her interests. She had a female teacher in middle school who showed her that math was fun and a science teacher who opened up the wide world of physics.

In Greece, as in much of Europe, students are expected to choose their area of study before they go to college. Kalogera chose physics. "Once I got into college for physics," she said, "I got more and more exposed to astronomy and astrophysics, and that became a true passion. And I also discovered that people could be paid to actually do research; this wasn't something that my family was aware of, or that I was aware of! So this was when I realized I could go to graduate school and pursue research."

After Kalogera graduated from the Aristotle University of Thessaloniki (Greece) in 1992, she went to graduate school at the University of Illinois at Urbana-Champaign, where she studied compact objects. After receiving her PhD in 1997, she continued her research at the Harvard-Smithsonian Center for Astrophysics, where she learned of LIGO.

At the time, the project was a physics experiment to detect gravitational waves as a way of confirming Einstein's general theory of relativity. "It was not thought widely as a new way of doing astronomy," she said. "Most people were doubtful and dismissive, and thought that it would never really happen. . . . So at the time I decided to join the LIGO project, I was not encouraged by my mentors. But I was really curious about it . . . so I just dipped my toe into the LIGO collaboration." Kalogera has become one of LIGO's most senior astrophysicists, riding gravitational waves to new frontiers in astronomy.

If they are very massive, like orbiting or colliding black holes, they send out gravitational waves in space-time, much as a stone tossed into a pond creates ripples in the water.

The LIGO discovery was not only the first time physicists were able to prove the existence of gravitational waves. It was also the first experimental evidence for binary black holes. As the black holes orbited around each other, gravitational forces pulled them closer and closer together until they finally merged in a colossal collision that LIGO was able to capture.

A SIGNAL DELIVERS A LOT OF BANG FOR THE BUCK

The LIGO scientists gained an astounding amount of information from the signal. They could tell that the two colliding black holes had twenty-nine times and thirty-six times the mass of the sun, respectively. In the final, furious moments before the collision, the black holes orbited each other 35 times per second. As they moved closer, their orbital speed shot up to 250 times per second before finally merging. The combined black hole had a mass of about sixty-two times the sun's mass, a little less than the combined mass of both black holes. The "missing" mass was released as a result of the force of the collision, and it took the form of gravitational wave energy. So about three times the mass of the sun (13 million trillion trillion pounds, or 6 million trillion trillion kg) was converted into gravitational wave energy. That is more than ten times the combined light energy of every star and galaxy in the observable universe!

DARK MATTER?

One of the great scientific mysteries is the nature of the matter and energy that make up our universe. Less than 5 percent of the universe is made of ordinary matter—the stuff we can actually detect, such as the protons, neutrons, and electrons that make up atoms. The rest of the universe is made of dark energy (68 percent) and dark matter (27 percent).

Dark matter is nearly impossible to detect because it does not absorb, reflect, or give off light in any part of the electromagnetic spectrum. But scientists know that dark matter is out there because things happen in the universe that can't be explained without the existence of something like dark matter. For example, the galaxies and galaxy clusters in our universe are rotating at great speed. The gravity generated by the matter we can observe in those galaxies—matter such as protons and neutrons—is simply not enough to hold them together. According to

scientific theory, the matter we can see *should* fly apart, scattering stars and gas. But it doesn't. So some type of matter must be exerting enough gravitational pull to keep the matter together.

Dark energy is even more mysterious. Scientists think this form of energy is embedded in the space-time fabric. In theory, the force of gravity should be slowing the expansion of the universe. But the redshifts in distant galaxies indicate that the universe is actually expanding faster and faster. Scientists think that dark energy may be behind the increasingly fast expansion of the universe.

MAMA BEARS

Various theories try to explain dark matter and dark energy. One theory says that our understanding of gravity may be wrong. Another theory suggests that dark energy may be a previously unidentified force in nature. Most theories predict that dark matter is made of some as-yet-undetected particle. Several experiments are under way at detectors to either create or look for these particles.

LIGO's results have at least one scientist thinking that a type of black hole known as a primordial (very first) black hole might be the elusive dark matter. Scientists haven't proven that primordial black holes are actually a real thing. But if they do exist, they formed in the first thousandths of a second after the big bang. They weren't created from stars, like stellar black holes, because stars didn't exist yet. Scientists think that primordial black holes formed from the collapse of great big balls of gas.

The first two black holes LIGO discovered are too large to fit the predictions of the mass of most stellar black holes. But they're too small to fit the predictions for supermassive black holes such as Sagittarius A*, at the center of our galaxy. These "Mama Bear" black holes—neither too big nor too small—might be primordial black holes.

Alexander Kashlinsky, an astrophysicist at NASA, has suggested that primordial black holes could account for the "missing" dark matter. He estimates that dark matter could be entirely accounted for with three trillion solar masses' worth of black holes.

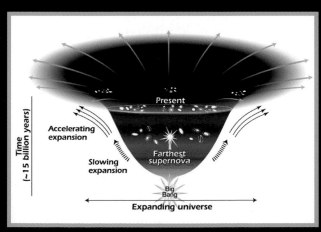

This diagram reveals changes in the rate of expansion since the universe's birth fifteen billion years ago. Astronomers theorize that the faster expansion rate is due to a mysterious, dark force that is pushing galaxies apart.

The LIGO scientists didn't have to wait long to find a second black hole collision. On December 26, 2015, just as many scientists were home enjoying the holidays with their families, the detectors picked up the strong signal of yet another black hole collision, 1.4 billion light-years away. These black holes were smaller—just 7.5 and 14.2 times the mass of the sun. While the first signal in September had lasted 0.2 seconds, the second one in December lasted a full second. LIGO had also recorded the final twenty-seven orbits of the black holes before they crashed into each other. The merger of the two

This illustration shows a simulation of two galaxies—each with supermassive black holes in the middle—in the process of merging. The black holes orbit each other for hundreds of millions of years before they merge to form a single supermassive black hole that sends out intense gravitational waves.

black holes released only one solar mass of energy. The fact that these two events happened so close in time is a strong indication that black hole collisions are much more common than scientists had originally thought.

Kalogera is excited about the LIGO discoveries. They make her even more passionate about learning how binary black hole systems form. Astrophysicists have two models to describe the formation of these systems. One model says that two similar stars are formed from the same cloud of gas, like identical twins splitting from the same egg in their mother's womb. The twin stars grow up together, orbiting each other throughout their lives in relative peace. When they exhaust their nuclear fuel, they explode into supernovas and collapse into black holes. The binary stars become binary black holes.

The second model says that the two stars formed independently but inside the same cluster of stars. Inside that cluster, the more massive stars move toward the center and become black holes. They eventually dance around each other before finally colliding and merging into binary black holes. Kalogera hopes that LIGO data will help determine which model is correct.

HOW DID LIGO DETECT GRAVITATIONAL WAVES?

It's very likely that gravitational waves pass through our bodies all the time. But since gravity is a weak force in the universe, we don't feel a thing. A passing gravitational wave might change the distance between you and the person sitting next to you by about a millionth of the diameter of a proton. It would take an awfully sensitive instrument to detect a gravitational wave. In fact, Einstein doubted scientists would ever be able to detect them.

The LIGO scientists decided to give it a go. They spent decades planning and constructing two observatories, each one functioning like an exquisitely sensitive pair of rulers. One is in Hanford, Washington, and the other is in Livingston, Louisiana, 1,865 miles (3,002 km) away. The LIGO team put the two detectors far apart on purpose. This way, they could tell whether a little jiggle was due to local vibrations only or to a gravitational wave from outer space. It would also allow them to get a general sense of the direction from which the wave came. Each observatory has an L-shaped vacuum tube, from which a vacuum pump has removed all air and other gases. Each arm of the tube is of equal length, a little more than 3.2 feet (1 m) wide and 2.5 miles (4 km) long. The arms are so long that project engineers had to raise them by 3.2 feet at each end so that they lay flat above Earth's curvature below.

A computer-controlled laser beam at the crook of the two arms is split into two. Each beam shoots down and hits a mirror at the end of the arm. The mirror sends the light bouncing back to the source at the crook of the arms. The speed of light in a vacuum is constant, so the beams should return to the source at the same time. Unless, that is, a gravitational wave ripples through LIGO's arms. Then one arm of the L would be stretched out while the other would be squeezed short. Since the beam in the stretched arm would have to travel a longer distance than the one in the squeezed arm, the two beams would arrive back at the source at different times. The strength of the gravitational wave would dictate this difference in time. So a mild gravitational wave would lead to only a slight difference in the time it took both beams of light to return. A stronger wave would create a greater difference in the timing.

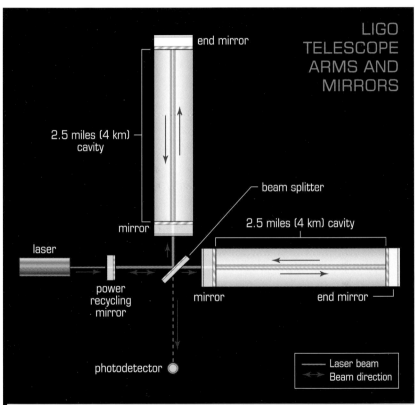

LIGO TELESCOPE ARMS AND MIRRORS

end mirror

2.5 miles (4 km) cavity

beam splitter

2.5 miles (4 km) cavity

mirror

laser

power recycling mirror

mirror

end mirror

photodetector

——— Laser beam
◄—► Beam direction

Each arm of the LIGO observatory is 2.5 miles (4 km) long. This infographic shows how mirrors and a beam splitter direct the light beams in the arms. Changes in the behavior of the light waves indicate an interaction with gravitational waves.

The LIGO instruments are supersensitive. They detect all sorts of sound vibrations from nearby traffic, earthquakes, and even distant ocean waves. To filter out all that noise, the team outfitted each detector with complex suspension systems, like sophisticated versions of those in a car, to insulate against outside vibrations.

"GRAVITY'S MUSIC"

In September 2015, after years of hard work, the LIGO scientists finally declared that the observatory was ready to detect gravitational waves. It didn't take long for the first signal to arrive, first at the Louisiana detector and seven milliseconds later at the Washington site. The "chirp" announced the passage of the gravitational wave across the continent.

Gravitational waves are not actually sound or light waves. You can't hear or see them, so there is no literal chirp. So the LIGO scientists devised a way of converting gravitational waves to sound waves. The technology is something like the way a mechanical wave you create by plucking a string on an electric guitar can be converted to sound with an amplifier. When the LIGO team first converted the gravitational wave to a sound wave, it sounded like the thump of a heartbeat. If the team shifted the frequency to make the wave easier to hear, it sounded a bit like a raindrop falling into a bucket of water. LIGO scientist Gabriela González, speaking at a press conference in San Diego, called it "gravity's music." You can go online and hear the sounds of the collision at LIGO's website at https://www.ligo.caltech.edu/video/ligo20160211v2.

Ultimately, the LIGO collaboration would like to

team up with other astronomers to use X-ray, radio, and visible light telescopes to further study colliding black holes. If telescope astronomy creates a silent movie version of colliding black holes, pairing it with LIGO's soundtrack will give scientists a more complete understanding of the event. The main challenge is that the two LIGO detectors aren't very good yet at pinpointing the source of the gravitational waves they pick up. That the September signal came first to the Louisiana site and then to the Washington site indicated only that the gravitational wave came from the Southern Hemisphere. It is difficult for astronomers to figure out exactly where to aim their telescopes if they are to coordinate their efforts.

> **"THE [LIGO] DETECTORS ACT MORE LIKE OUR EARS, AND LESS LIKE OUR EYES. OUR EYES ARE LIKE REGULAR TELESCOPES; WE POINT WITH OUR EYES. IN CONTRAST, OUR EARS CAN HEAR SOUNDS THAT COME FROM IN BACK OF US, FROM UNDER THE FLOOR, IN ALL DIRECTIONS."**
>
> *—VICKY KALOGERA*

"The [LIGO] detectors act more like our ears, and less like our eyes," Kalogera says. "Our eyes are like regular telescopes; we point with our eyes. In contrast, our ears can hear sounds that come from in back of us, from under the floor, in all directions."

DO YOU USE
YOUR PHONE'S GPS SYSTEM TO GET AROUND? YOU CAN THANK EINSTEIN!

For many of us, the Global Positioning System (GPS) is part of our everyday lives. We use it on our smartphones to find our friends, the nearest pizza parlor, and to play games. Originally developed for military navigation, GPS is based on an array of approximately thirty-two satellites orbiting Earth. No matter where you are on Earth, you are reachable by at least four of those satellites. At frequent intervals, each one sends radio signals about its position and its current time. Once your GPS device picks up signals from at least three satellites, it can pinpoint your location on Earth, to within about 49 feet (15 m).

On board, each GPS satellite has an atomic clock (a superaccurate clock that runs on atomic vibrations). Einstein's general theory of relativity predicts that as gravitational pull becomes stronger, the more time will appear to slow down. So the satellite clocks in space, where the gravitational pull is weaker, will seem to run faster than those on Earth. Yet special relativity also says that the satellite's clocks are moving relative to a clock on Earth, so they will actually seem to run slower. Taken together—the effects of gravity plus the relative relationship between space clocks and Earth clocks—the overall result is that time on a GPS satellite clock runs faster than a clock on Earth by about thirty-eight microseconds each day. That may not sound like much, but without making the proper adjustments for time, the GPS coordinates for where you are on Earth would be off by at least 6 miles (10 km) each day. We'd be lost without general relativity!

The US Air Force maintains GPS satellites in orbit around Earth. They fly at an altitude of around 12,550 miles (20,200 km). Each satellite circles Earth twice a day, sending radio signals to users. This G lock IIIA will be the most current generation of GPS satellites. It is projected to launch in 2018.

After LIGO detected gravitational waves from two colliding black holes, scientists from Johns Hopkins University's Department of Physics and Astronomy published a hypothesis that the LIGO discovery could be a signature of dark matter. This image, using data from the Chandra and Hubble telescopes in 2012, shows the distribution of dark matter, galaxies, and hot gas in the core of the merging galaxy cluster Abell 520. The cluster was formed from a violent collision of massive galaxy clusters about 2.4 billion light-years from Earth.

A larger network of detectors, Kalogera says, could work together to help scientists zero in on the source of the gravitational waves, much as a collection of satellites helps GPS systems pinpoint a location on Earth.

LIGO can only detect gravitational waves within a certain range of frequencies. But different sources in the cosmos emit gravitational waves with different frequencies. Other detectors can be designed to pick up waves with higher and lower frequencies. A collection of gravitational wave detectors could "hear" the entire orchestra of music from the cosmos, from the high-frequency waves of binary neutron star systems to the low-frequency rumble of a supermassive black hole.

Scientists plan to build a third LIGO observatory in India, and Japan is building an underground one. Italy and Germany have smaller detectors similar to LIGO. These may become part of a larger network of gravitational wave detectors. Scientists from six nations are working to launch, in 2034, three networked space-based observatories that could detect very low-frequency gravitational waves.

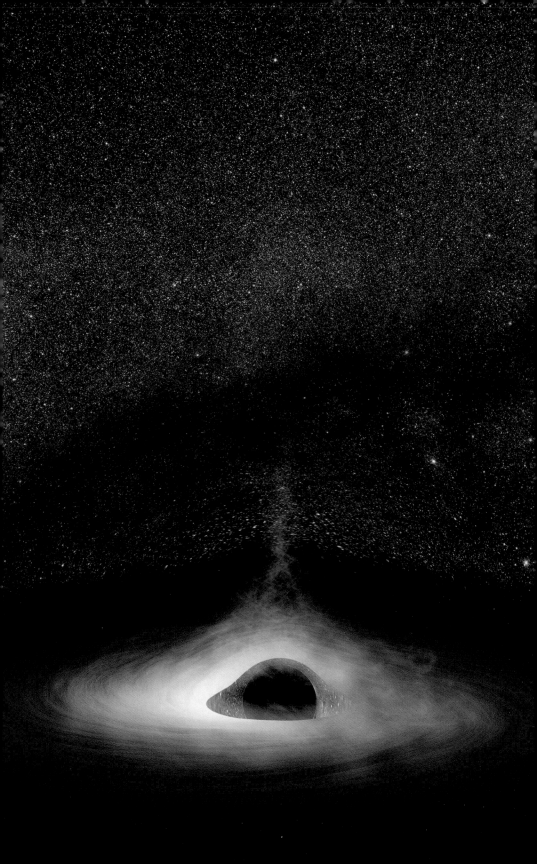

4

WHAT'S ON THE (EVENT) HORIZON?

Everyone knows that it's impossible to see black holes, right? We've observed the effects they have on nearby stars and gases. We've detected the gravitational waves that come crashing through the universe when black holes collide. We've seen jets of energy that belch from ravenously feeding black holes. Although scientists have seen blurry images that *suggest* the presence of a black hole, we've never really, truly seen one.

A group of scientists from around the world is hoping to capture an image of the black hole Sagittarius A*—or more precisely, its event horizon—at the center of the Milky Way galaxy.

They've also got their sights set on a monster black hole, estimated at six billion times the mass of the sun, in a galaxy known as Messier 87 (M87). This galaxy is at the center of the cluster of galaxies in the Virgo constellation of stars, about 50 million light-years away. The M87 black hole is much farther away from us than Sagittarius A*, and it's also a whole lot larger. An image of the event horizon of either black hole would be the most direct evidence to date of the existence of black holes.

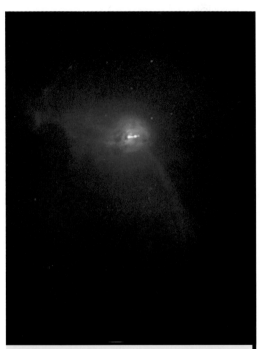

This is a combined image from two Chandra observations of the giant elliptical galaxy Messier 87—50 million light-years from Earth. Bright arcs and dark cavities in the multimillion-degree-Celsius atmosphere of M87 surround a central jet. Much farther out, two plumes extend beyond the rings. These features, plus radio observations, show that repetitive outbursts from the central supermassive black hole have been affecting the entire galaxy for at least one hundred million years. Scientists believe that outbursts from supermassive black holes in giant galaxies may be common. They may determine how fast giant galaxies and their central black holes grow.

Scientists are starting with Sagittarius A*. They have calculated that it would appear as a dark circle in the middle of a gas cloud in the constellation Sagittarius at the center of the Milky Way. Its tremendous gravity will distort and magnify any image scientists take, sort of like the distortions of a funhouse mirror. So scientists would expect to see a shadow of the black hole about 50 million miles (80.5 million km) wide.

Sagittarius A* is so compact and so very far away that getting a good look at it would be like someone on Earth trying to take a picture of a grapefruit sitting on the moon. You would need a very large telescope to get enough focus and clarity to see the grapefruit.

A radio telescope is the ideal instrument to look more closely at Sagittarius A*. (Radio telescopes, like other telescopes, detect electromagnetic waves from sources in space—in this case, radio waves.) Because radio waves are very long, they can pierce through Earth's atmosphere and through the galactic dust between Earth and the center of the Milky Way galaxy. Visible wavelengths can't do that. Scientists also believe that the hot gas at the Sagittarius A* event horizon will shine brightly when the high-frequency (0.05 inches, or 1.3 millimeter) radio wavelengths hit the gas.

However, to get the kind of resolution needed to see the event horizon of Sagittarius A*, scientists would need an Earth-sized radio telescope. That's impossible. So the next best thing is a network of nine radio telescopes situated around the world: the Event Horizon Telescope (EHT). The trick—and it's not a small one—is getting all the telescopes to work together, looking at the same object at the exact same time, and coordinating all the data to create a single high-resolution image.

In 2005 a team of astronomers led by Zhiqiang Shen of the Shanghai Astronomical Observatory in China caught a fuzzy glimpse of Sagittarius A*. The team used an array of ten radio telescopes stretching from Hawaii to the Caribbean island of Saint Croix (one of the US Virgin Islands). Known as the Very Long Baseline Array (VLBA), the networked telescopes provided data to create an image showing that the diameter of Sagittarius A* was less than 90 million miles (145 million km) across—less than Earth's distance from the sun. Ionized electrons and protons in space blurred the image, however, and the black hole's event horizon appeared larger than scientists expected. This is not unlike the way frosted glass blurs and enlarges the image of something on the other side of the pane of glass.

EHT scientists hope to sharpen that blurry image. The EHT telescopes are all over the world, which gives

Scientists check for ice on the dish of the Large Millimeter Telescope (LMT) Alfonso Serrano. The LMT is part of a network of radio telescopes known as the Event Horizon Telescope. The LMT sits atop a dormant volcano in Mexico, at an altitude of 15,092 feet (4,600 m).

EHT images much better resolution than VLBA images. And the additional EHT radio telescopes will be tuned to slightly higher radio frequencies so that the waves can more effectively make their way through the cosmic haze.

Radio astronomy is not always easy. Water vapor in Earth's atmosphere absorbs radio waves, so radio observatories tend to be built at high, dry places. Still, powerful storms do sometimes roll in at these high elevations, making observing difficult to impossible. And because radio signals sent far into space are very weak, it's important to filter out as much radio frequency noise from Earth as possible. It's like tuning a radio to get rid of the static between stations. The more remote and the quieter the location, the better for radio astronomy!

One of the most powerful radio telescopes on Earth is the Atacama Large Millimeter/submillimeter Array (ALMA). It is in the Atacama Desert of Chile on a 16,400-foot (5,000 m) plateau, one of the driest places on Earth. Filmmakers use it as a location to shoot scenes that are meant to take place on Mars. In fact, scientists have found that the soil of the Atacama Desert is just as lifeless as that on the surface of Mars. And because the plateau is at such a high altitude, oxygen levels are low. Scientists and engineers working at the ALMA site wear portable oxygen tanks to avoid passing out. They are allowed to spend just six hours a day at this high altitude.

ALMA is actually made of many small antennae that are 40 feet (12 m) in diameter. The antennae combine data to work together as a single large telescope. The ambitious goal of the EHT team is to network ALMA with other independent radio observatories in similarly remote and forbidding places across the world. This requires a mind-boggling degree of coordination. For example, on an agreed-upon observation night, scientists at each telescope point their dishes at Sagittarius A*. Each telescope has an atomic clock. The clocks are synchronized to an extreme level of accuracy—only a one-second shift every one hundred million years. The telescopes track the black hole throughout the night, using Earth's rotation to view it at different angles. The telescopes store data on hard drives, shipping them off to MIT. There, a supercomputer puts all the data together for analysis.

CHIRP

Coordinating the information from each observatory is tricky. Katie Bouman, a graduate student in electrical engineering and computer science at MIT, explained how the telescopes work together. Imagine, she said, "that

The Event Horizon Telescope

A network of telescopes as big as Earth is trying to measure the boundary of what astronomers suspect is a supermassive black hole at the center of our Milky Way galaxy. Placing the telescopes as far apart as possible increases the array's ability to discern small details and increases the resolution of the resulting images.

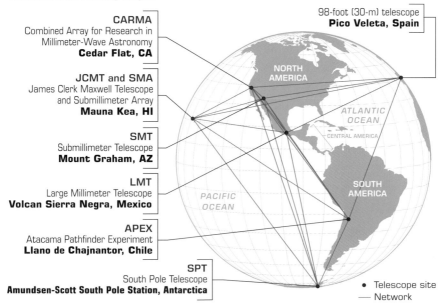

CARMA
Combined Array for Research in Millimeter-Wave Astronomy
Cedar Flat, CA

98-foot (30-m) telescope
Pico Veleta, Spain

NORTH AMERICA

JCMT and SMA
James Clerk Maxwell Telescope and Submillimeter Array
Mauna Kea, HI

ATLANTIC OCEAN

CENTRAL AMERICA

SMT
Submillimeter Telescope
Mount Graham, AZ

LMT
Large Millimeter Telescope
Volcan Sierra Negra, Mexico

SOUTH AMERICA

PACIFIC OCEAN

APEX
Atacama Pathfinder Experiment
Llano de Chajnantor, Chile

SPT
South Pole Telescope
Amundsen-Scott South Pole Station, Antarctica

• Telescope site
— Network

you have a big pond. You and your friend are sitting very far apart on the shore at the edges of the pond. There are a bunch of frogs jumping up and down in the center of the pond, which causes ripples. You can't see the frogs; you can only see the waves as they approach you at the shore."

Bouman points out that you can measure the wave patterns that reach you and compare them to the patterns that reach your friend a little farther away. The ripples, or waves, will interfere with one another. Some will amplify the waves to form crests (peaks). Some will cancel them out, forming troughs (low points or valleys). By merging your information about the waves in the water, you can figure out where the frogs are.

Similarly, the radio telescopes are like you and your friend at the edge of the pond. Scientists can study the data they receive from the radio waves emitted by a black hole. From the waves, they can then create an image of the black hole at the center of our galaxy. It's a technique called interferometry. It's a powerful tool for merging data from different telescopes.

The EHT scientists face some additional challenges in creating an image of Sagittarius A*. Radio waves from cosmic sources usually reach any two telescopes on Earth at slightly different times. Earth's atmosphere can slow them down, exaggerating differences in arrival time and throwing off the calculations needed to merge the information from the two telescopes.

Bouman developed a new algorithm (a process or set of rules to be followed in calculations) that she calls Continuous High-resolution Image Reconstruction using Patch priors (CHIRP) to address that problem.

PROFILE:
KATIE BOUMAN

Katie Bouman got her first real taste of the thrill of scientific research in sixth grade with her first science fair project at West Lafayette, Indiana. It was supposed to be a tiny project, she said. But instead, she baked three hundred loaves of bread to study the rising effects of yeast on dough. Her efforts paid off, and she won the gold medal in her category.

When she was a junior in high school, Bouman found herself with an empty slot in her class schedule. A friend urged her to take a programming class. Bouman balked. "Programming sounds boring and stupid," she told her friend. But the friend persisted, convincing her that she could do some cool projects. "So I took it, and I feel like that was really the start of when I seriously got into research," she said. "I got an offer to be a research assistant for the summer in an image processing lab [in her hometown at Purdue University]."

When she graduated from high school in 2007, she went to college at the University of Michigan in Ann Arbor to study electrical engineering. She found that she really liked working with images. "You can see your results. I can visualize what's going on, and I really enjoy that," she said. She went to graduate school at MIT to continue her studies in image processing and electrical engineering.

Her research adviser at MIT told her about a project called the Event Horizon Telescope. She had a casual interest in astronomy as a girl, but she didn't know a lot about it. She suspected, though, that this project just might offer her the image processing challenge she was looking for. "At first I was really working on the project alone," she said. She took what she learned from textbooks and tried to come up with a new algorithm for imaging a black hole. "It's difficult if you don't know the details of the specific physics. . . . It's a big learning curve."

A high school computer programming class opened Katie Bouman's eyes to the possibilities of image processing and electrical engineering.

So she went to a meeting about black holes to try to learn more. "It was a really cool experience; I got to hear all these physicists debating about whether the black hole at the center of our galaxy has a jet or not, crazy things like that," she said. "It was a very different world than the one I live in, engineering. It was kind of like something out of a movie. But I met a lot of good astronomers who really took me under their wing, and I've been working closely with them since.

"I'd like to continue with astronomy, but I'm not limited to it," she continued. "I just really like the computational imaging problems where you pull out the hidden signal." You can watch Katie Bouman's TEDx talk, "How to Take a Picture of a Black Hole," at https://www.ted.com/talks/katie_bouman_what_does_a_black_hole_look_like.

It multiplies the data from three telescopes to cancel out the delays caused by Earth's atmosphere.

CHIRP solves another problem for the EHT. With just a few telescopes scattered across Earth, the EHT data is incomplete. Scientists can use the data to make any number of images of the black hole. The images could all match the data but not necessarily be a true reflection of the black hole.

"This [situation of incomplete data creating an image] poses a real conundrum, because we've never seen a black hole," Bouman said. "We have some idea of what a black hole might look like, but we don't want to impose too much prior information on that. We don't want to get into a circular argument where we're reconstructing something that we expected to see."

CHIRP helps create an image that both fits the data and agrees with what we already know about black holes. To do this, Bouman fed a huge database of real-world images, from pictures of galaxies to cats and houses, into the computer's algorithm. "Even though there's a huge variation in these kinds of images, if you break them up into 64-pixel patches [small visual units], there's a lot in common," she explained. Over time, the computer learned which patches come together in a way that produces an image that best fits the data. "When we're trying to reconstruct an image of the black hole, we're treating those little patches [of galaxy images] as puzzle pieces, fitting them together in a collage to make an image that's likely, based on what we know about images in general."

If everything goes well, EHT scientists hope to see a clear picture of the Sagittarius A* black hole emerge sometime in 2017. So far, they have already taken terabytes (one terabyte is one million million bytes) of radio frequency data, and they will continue to take many more. You can follow the project at http://www.eventhorizontelescope.org/.

A THEORY (POSSIBLY) CONFIRMED

What's the scientific payoff for the EHT? It's not just that scientists want to create pretty pictures of some of the most mysterious objects in the universe, although that would be fantastic. EHT will provide a laboratory of sorts to test the predictions and limits of Einstein's general theory of relativity. For example, his theory predicts that the strong curvature of space-time near a black hole will produce a dark shadow surrounded by a bright ring of photons. If scientists do capture an image of the event horizon shadow, it will be a major confirmation of the theory.

Just as exciting is the prospect of watching Sagittarius A* dine, perhaps on a blob of gas. We would expect to see the gas orbit the event horizon at nearly the speed of light and watch its last moments before it is swallowed into the black hole. The fast-moving gas should emit light from a particular place in the black hole, giving scientists a great tool for measuring how light and matter are affected by extreme gravity.

Sagittarius A* is a picky eater, as black holes go. It's on a near-starvation diet. The gigantic M87 black hole in Virgo, on the other hand, is a much less picky and messier eater. It has swallowed an entire medium-sized galaxy over the past billion years and regularly burps out huge jets of energy into the universe. One day EHT scientists hope to capture an image of this black hole too!

5

BLACK HOLES JUST WANNA HAVE FUN

Orbiting high above Earth, one-third of the way to the moon, is the Chandra X-ray Observatory satellite. The observatory is named in honor of Indian American Nobel prize-winning astrophysicist Subrahmanyan Chandrasekhar (or, Chandra, which means "moon" or "luminous" in Sanskrit). In 1930, when he was just nineteen years old, he calculated that white dwarf stars could not exceed a certain mass—now accepted to be around 1.4 times the mass of the sun. Once the dying star exceeded this limit, which came to be known as the Chandrasekhar limit, the object would no longer be able to resist the force of gravity.

It would explode in a fiery supernova. The remote-controlled Chandra observatory carries a telescope specially designed to detect X-rays from very hot regions in the universe: supernovas, galaxy clusters, and the stuff around black holes.

In 2015 Eric Schlegel, an astrophysicist at the University of Texas in San Antonio, was looking at some archived data from Chandra. It showed a small galaxy, NGC 5195, merging with a much larger spiral galaxy NGC 5194. Spiral galaxies are named for their distinct spiral shape, in which stars, gas, and dust are gathered in spiral arms that spread outward from the center. Located 26 million light-years away, in the Hunting Dogs constellation, the larger galaxy is nicknamed the Whirlpool because of its curving spiral arms. Like a whirlpool, it is slowly drawing its companion galaxy into its center. This little dance has been going on for hundreds of millions of years. The Whirlpool will eventually swallow its smaller partner.

Schlegel noticed two boomerang-shaped arcs of X-ray emission close to the center of NGC 5195, the smaller of the two galaxies. The arcs, Schlegel and his colleagues guessed, indicate burps of gas from the Whirlpool. The curves mapped right back to the home of the black hole at the center of the galaxy. Because of the amount of belched gas, Schlegel thinks that a lot of matter must have been dumped very quickly into the black hole at the center of the Whirlpool—and been kicked out just as quickly. It's as though you chugged a soda much too fast. Like the Whirlpool, you belch a lot of gas quickly after drinking the soda.

The X-ray arcs represent cosmic fossils from two enormous blasts from the Whirlpool that happened

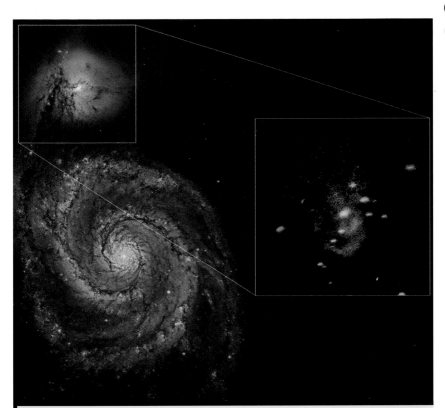

These images from Chandra and Hubble show two merging galaxies (NGC 5195, *top left*, and NGC 5194, *bottom left*) within the larger Messier 51 galaxy. The bright whitish-blue outburst at the center of the blue inset at right is the galaxy's supermassive black hole. Two boomerang-shaped arcs below it are burps of gas from NGC 5194.

millions of years ago. The arcs of X-ray emissions would have taken one to six million years to reach their current positions. The radiation would have taken another twenty-six million years to reach us.

That was interesting enough, but then Schlegel compared the emissions to some twenty-year-old data of the same region. These were from an optical telescope at the Kitt Peak National Observatory in Arizona. In the older image, he found two slender emission lines of relatively cool hydrogen gas just outside the X-ray arcs. Together, the X-ray and optical images told a story. As the two X-ray shocks traveled outward, they snowplowed hydrogen gas from the center of the NGC 5195 galaxy off to the sides. "Thank goodness for archives," he said. "It was picture perfect." The images clearly supported the hypothesis that black holes do indeed belch. In fact, Schlegel thought he must have been cherry-picking the data. He wondered if he was acknowledging only the evidence that supports a hypothesis—and ignoring the rest. "I'd never seen anything work out that well," he said. "Usually, if you're at the edge of a research frontier, there's a lot of noise. You spend a lot of time squinting and thinking, 'Is this really something?'"

Schlegel walked away from the data for a couple of days and then came back. He carefully walked through every step of the data and came to the same conclusion. The X-ray burps had indeed plowed through hydrogen gas at the center of the galaxy, pushing the gas to the outer edges. This hydrogen gas was a stellar nursery!

If you live in a part of the country with snowplows, you've seen the huge mounds of snow they form at the sides of the road. Just as snow plowed to the edges of the street can form dense snow-packed hills, the X-ray blast waves created areas of hydrogen gas dense enough to form stars farther from the center of the galaxy. And Schlegel and his team have found what appear to be new stars forming at the outer edge of the blast wave from the Whirlpool.

Schlegel and others believe this kind of black hole behavior probably happened very often in the early universe. The black holes shaped the evolving structures of galaxies. But it's rare to catch them in the act. "If you look at a true color image of a spiral galaxy, you immediately see that the outskirts are relatively blue in color," Schlegel said, "and the nuclear [interior] region is relatively orange." That blue radiation tells us that stars in the outskirts are younger, because young stars tend to be more massive and hot, and stars tend to form on the arms of spiral galaxies.

The orange stars in the interior pose more of a puzzle, Schlegel said. Stars don't seem to be forming there. "You could just imagine that you've got older stars [in the interior], but we think that galaxies are formed at roughly the same time. The stars in the nuclear region ought to be roughly the same age as stars out our way." (Our solar system is roughly halfway between the center of the Milky Way and its outer edge.) But they're not. Stars in the nuclear region appear to be older than stars closer to us. And the reason why, Schlegel said, is probably because the black hole has blown the gas that could have been used to form new stars into the outer parts of the galaxy.

This kind of behavior, which astronomers call feedback, is the way our universe helps regulate the size of a black hole and of the galaxy itself. "Otherwise," Schlegel said, a black hole that keeps eating and picking up new matter "could become large enough to engulf a galaxy." So black holes not only consume new matter, but they also spit out and create new things.

"DOUBLE BUBBLE TROUBLE"

Sagittarius A*, the black hole at the center of the Milky Way, is relatively quiet, but it wasn't always. In fact, it's likely that millions of years ago "our" black hole blew two huge bubbles.

PROFILE: ERIC SCHLEGEL

Many successful people—scientists, artists, and entrepreneurs—can identify an aha moment in their lives that steered them toward their chosen fields. Not Eric Schlegel. It's not because he hasn't thought about it. He has—a lot. He even went into hypnotherapy (a type of therapy that explores the mind through hypnosis) to try to figure out why he'd been interested in astronomy from a very young age. No dice. It seems he was simply born an astronomer.

He had the good fortune of growing up in eastern Pennsylvania and Maryland, where he could see clear night skies unpolluted by city lights. His father worked for the Boy Scouts, maintaining campsites year-round. There, he had plenty of opportunities to stargaze. His high school had a planetarium, which furthered his interest in astronomy.

Schlegel studied astronomy at the State University of New York at Albany. Then went to graduate school at Indiana University—Bloomington, earning a PhD in 1983. During those years of study, his focus on astronomy and astrophysics never wavered. Schlegel teaches and does research at the University of Texas in San Antonio, where he has studied supernovas, binary stars, and galaxies. They are all related, he says, because "you can go from one to the next, and each one has an impact on the one that follows it."

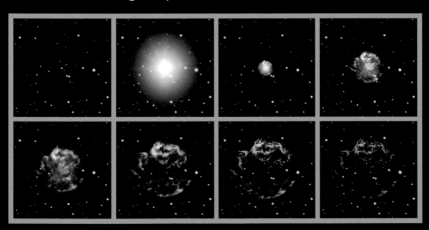

Eric Schlegel studies supernovas such as these.

They extended tens of thousands of light-years above the disk-shaped Milky Way.

In 2009 astrophysicist Douglas Finkbeiner of Harvard University was looking for dark matter in the Milky Way. He and other scientists saw a mysterious microwave haze in the inner part of the galaxy. Perhaps, they thought, the haze was dark matter, pulled in toward the center of the galaxy by gravity. If dark matter particles collided with one another in the crowded core of the Milky Way, Finkbeiner thought, they would create high-energy charged particles and gamma rays.

Finkbeiner turned to recently released data from the Fermi Gamma-ray Space Telescope, a space observatory in low-Earth orbit. The NASA telescope, launched in 2008, scans the entire sky 24-7, 365 days a year, searching for the highest energy form of light: gamma rays. Finkbeiner and his colleagues found a lot of gamma rays in the inner part of the Milky Way galaxy, all right. As they analyzed the data, they began to see that the gamma rays were arranged in a big figure eight extending above and below the disk of the Milky Way. The figure eight looked like twin teardrop bubbles anchored one on top of the other at the galaxy's core. According to computer models, dark matter wouldn't do that. It would form a spherical halo. At first, Finkbeiner was disappointed. He told colleagues he had "double bubble trouble."

Finkbeiner soon realized they hadn't discovered dark matter. But they had stumbled onto something very interesting. The team named the gamma ray bubbles Fermi Bubbles, after the telescope they had used to find them. (The telescope itself is named after twentieth-century Italian American physicist Enrico Fermi. He helped build the world's first nuclear reactor, among other accomplishments.)

What could the bubbles be? Scientists had discovered bubbles in other galaxies, especially galaxies with supermassive black holes one hundred or even one thousand times the mass of the black hole at the center of the Milky Way. Sagittarius A* is puny in comparison. It is a black hole of only four million solar masses. Up until then, it had the reputation among astronomers as a quiet wallflower among the louder, more boisterous black holes in the universe. With Finkbeiner's discovery in 2009, it seems that Sagittarius A* may have seen some wilder times, perhaps as recently as the last one hundred thousand years.

"When stuff falls into that black hole, as you can imagine, it makes a big mess," Finkbeiner told *Scientific American*. "One of the things that happens is very high-energy particles get ejected, and probably shock waves, and you can get jets of material coming off of the thing." Those jets might well have formed the Fermi Bubbles.

Another possibility is that a burst of star births and deaths in the inner galaxy occurred, probably within the last ten million years. This flurry of activity could have propelled a great deal of radiation and matter outward, forming bubble-like structures.

It may be that the Fermi Bubbles were created by a combination of the two processes. Scientists have found evidence in other galaxies that when a black hole feeds, it leads to a burst of new star formation.

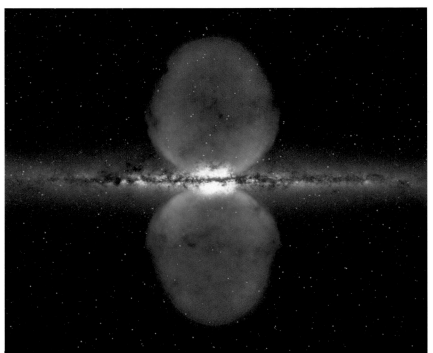

From end to end, the Fermi gamma ray bubbles discovered in 2009 extend 50,000 light-years, or roughly half of the Milky Way's diameter. X-rays (blue) from ROentgen SATellite (ROSAT) observatory, a Germany-led mission in the 1990s, are the edges of the bubbles. The gamma rays (magenta) mapped by Fermi extend much farther.

DO BLACK HOLES SING?

The Milky Way's Fermi Bubbles are impressive. But in a galactic bubble-blowing contest, our galaxy falls far short. About 250 million light-years away is Perseus, a gigantic galaxy cluster. Like most galaxy clusters, it is anchored by a huge black hole at its center. The Perseus cluster contains one thousand times the mass of the Milky Way and stretches across 12 million light-years. Much of that mass is really hot, up to tens of millions of degrees Fahrenheit. It glows with X-ray frequency photons. In fact, it's the brightest X-ray object in our neighborhood. It's a great place to do X-ray astronomy.

Andrew Fabian, an astronomer at the Institute of Astronomy in Cambridge, England, used the Chandra observatory to make a detailed study of the Perseus cluster. He saw something incredible: two huge, bubble-shaped cavities, each about 50,000 light-years wide, extending away from the central supermassive black hole. Those cavities, bright sources of radio waves, are packed with high-energy particles and magnetic fields. The cavities pushed aside hotter, X-ray emitting gas, creating ripples in space—actual sound waves. The period of each wave, from one peak of the wave to another, is about ten million years. Chandra had recorded a snapshot of these slow-moving waves.

The Perseus black hole sound waves are a sort of song. They sing at a very low bass register, in a range far lower than we could ever hear—a million billion times lower, to be exact. The black hole sings just one note: a B flat that is fifty-seven octaves below middle C on a piano. For a visual animation of the sound waves generated by the Perseus cluster black hole, visit http://chandra.harvard.edu/photo/2003/perseus /animations.html.

The black hole seems to be doing much more than just entertaining nearby galaxies with its musical abilities. For years, astronomers have been puzzled about why so much hot gas is in the inner regions of the Perseus cluster. That gas should have cooled over the past ten billion years, forming trillions of stars. But it hasn't. Why not?

Chandra observations suggest that the energy in the cavities is carried by the sound waves as they travel through the gas. That energy keeps the gas warm, preventing it from cooling. Every few million years, some gas starts to cool and condense, falling back in toward the black hole. The black hole feeds again, spitting out jets of matter once again, creating more bubbles and sound waves that send their rumbling energy outward into the gas. Those black hole bubbles seem to be serving as a thermostat for Perseus, keeping it at a steady hot temperature.

Perseus and the Milky Way aren't the only galaxy

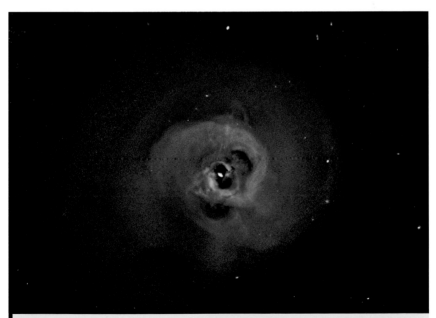

Galaxy clusters such as Perseus (*above*) are immersed in gas and are held together by gravity. Chandra observations of Perseus show that turbulence is preventing stars from forming there. The black hole at the center of this galaxy cluster pumps out huge amounts of energy through powerful jets of energetic particles. Chandra and other X-ray telescopes have detected giant cavities that the jets create in the hot cluster gas.

participants in the cosmic bubble-blowing contest. Astrophysicists have found evidence for bubbles in 70 percent of all galaxy clusters in the universe. They have found evidence for sound waves traveling through the bubble surrounding the giant galaxy M87 in the Virgo cluster. That black hole sings even lower than the Perseus black hole, with notes as low as fifty-nine octaves below middle C. Many scientists believe that

SOUND WAVES
IN SPACE?

Here on Earth, we can hear sound waves because they travel through some sort of medium, like air or water. They cause surrounding air or water molecules to vibrate, and these vibrations pass from one molecule to another. Our ears pick up the vibrations as sound.

So how do sound waves travel in space, which is a vacuum with neither air nor water? And can you even hear them?

Steven Allen, a professor of physics at Stanford University, explained that when black holes shoot out gas jets traveling at nearly the speed of light, they slam into the surrounding hot gas. "They beat a 'galactic drum,'" he told *Scientific American*. The jets are the sticks, and the surface of the gas is the drum. We can't hear these sound waves, because sound can't travel between the vacuum [that lies] between Perseus and us. But we can see them with X-rays. As the sound waves travel through the galaxy, we see the regions of greater pressure as sound wave peaks and the regions of weaker pressure as troughs.

these bubbles are yet another indication that black holes shape entire galaxies.

THE GREEN VALLEY OF THE UNIVERSE

In a 1970 song called "Woodstock," singer Joni Mitchell famously sang about humans being made of stardust. American astronomer Carl Sagan elaborated in a somewhat more scientific, yet still poetic way. He said, "The nitrogen in our DNA, the calcium in our teeth, the iron in our blood, the carbon in our apple pies were made in the interiors of collapsing stars. We are made of star-stuff."

Both Mitchell and Sagan are right. With the exception of hydrogen, which was made in the first few minutes after the big bang, the stuff (matter) we are made of comes out of dying stars that collapsed, went out in a blaze of supernova glory, and spewed new matter into the universe. We know that black holes, far from being simply greedy objects of destruction, can also regulate star formation and the structure of galaxies.

We can't say for sure that life on Earth (and possibly elsewhere) would *not* exist without black holes. But it's clear to scientists that the universe and its galaxies would be very different without at least some of them. They might not be very hospitable to life or at least to life as we know it.

For example, a galaxy anchored by a huge, voracious black hole would, over time, see little new star formation. And that means no carbon, oxygen, or other building blocks of life would be present. A galaxy with a slacker of a black hole, on the other hand, might create a lot of new stars. It might make massive stars that burn up in a hurry and explode, blasting away the atmosphere of any nearby planets. It wouldn't be a very friendly place for life.

Caleb Scharf is an astrobiologist at Columbia University in New York City. He argues that the black hole at the center of the Milky Way galaxy was instrumental in creating a place suitable for life in the place and time in which life on Earth exists. The Milky Way, he said, "is in something of a sweet spot. It is neither one of those old-looking galaxies, nor one churning out lots of new stars. It is in between, in what astronomers call the green valley: it is still making some stars but not at a rate that is hazardous to the development of complex structures."

SEEING THE UNSEEABLE

Long before Einstein published his general theory of relativity, John Michell proposed the existence of dark stars so dense that nothing, not even light, could escape their clutches. As if aware of the reaction he would get (what a preposterous idea!), he gave his paper a long, complex, and evasive title: "On the Means of Discovering the Distance, Magnitude, &c. of the Fixed Stars, in Consequence of the Diminution of the Velocity of Their Light, in Case Such a Diminution Should Be Found to Take Place in Any of Them, and Such Other Data Should be Procured from Observations, as Would Be Farther Necessary for That Purpose."

We know that although Michell got the details wrong, he had the right idea. Imagine what he might think if he could jump into a wormhole and travel to our time. Surely he would be delighted to join Andrea Ghez atop Mauna

Kea to watch the stars in their gravitational dance around Sagittarius A*. He would marvel at the gamma ray burst that announced the birth of a new black hole, the images of the burps and bubbles of black holes, and the music of gravitational waves. Michell, who designed and built his own telescopes, would be fascinated by the complexities of the many amazing telescopes—both optical and radio wave—that help us see the unseeable: the very edge of a black hole.

Equipped only with a homemade telescope and a top-notch brain, Michell came up with the rudimentary idea for black holes. In the two hundred-plus years since then, we have gained an incredible amount of knowledge about black holes. We can thank scientific advances in physics and astronomy, along with a technology boom that brought us increasingly sophisticated telescopes, detectors, and computers. And yet it seems clear that we could spend several more lifetimes studying black holes and working out what they can tell us about the way the universe works as a whole.

The current generation of telescopes and detectors, along with new ones in development, will be a source of scientifically rich data for years to come. Some of that data will probably be unexpected. It will probably lead to a deeper understanding of the laws of the universe. That's how science progresses. Maybe you, the reader, will be a part of it.

BLACK HOLES

Scientists believe the universe holds an enormous number of black holes. About one in one thousand stars have enough mass to become a black hole when it dies. The Milky Way galaxy alone could harbor up to one hundred million stellar-sized black holes. Presumably the hundreds of billions of galaxies in the universe have a similar number of stellar black holes. And we are pretty sure that a hulking supermassive black hole is at the center of all those galaxies. It is impossible to profile all the black holes in the universe. Here are some that scientists think are the most notable:

SAGITTARIUS A*

Type: Supermassive

Mass: About four million times the mass of the sun

Location: In the constellation Sagittarius, at the center
                 of the Milky Way galaxy, about 26,000 light-
                 years from Earth

What makes it
an all-star: Responsible for creating conditions favorable
                 to life on Earth

NGC 1600

Type: Supermassive

Mass: Seventeen billion times the mass of the sun

Location: In the constellation Eridanus, 200 million light-years from Earth

What makes it
an all-star: The biggest black hole discovered to date

J0100+2802

Type: Supermassive

Mass: About twelve to thirteen billion times the mass of the sun

Location: 12.8 billion light-years from Earth

What makes it
an all-star: Born about one billion years after the big bang; still puzzling to scientists about how it grew so large, so fast

GRS 1915+105 (AND ITS COMPANION STAR)

Type: Stellar

Mass: About fourteen times the mass of the sun

Location: In the constellation Aquila, about 40,000 light-years from Earth

What makes it an all-star: The fastest spinning black hole ever discovered, a whirling dervish that feeds off the material of its companion star, with material on the edge of its event horizon spinning at about 350 million miles (563 million km) per hour, or about half the speed of light

CYGNUS X-1

Type:	Stellar
Mass:	About 14.8 times the mass of the sun
Location:	In the constellation Cygnus, about 6,000 to 8,000 lightyears away from Earth
What makes it an all-star:	One of the first black holes scientists discovered; emits some of the strongest X-rays ever detected from Earth

IGR J17091

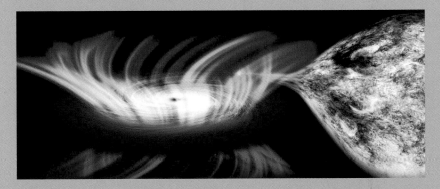

Type:	Stellar
Mass:	Less than three times the mass of the sun
Location:	In the Milky Way, about 28,000 light-years from Earth
What makes it an all-star:	The smallest black hole yet discovered, near the theoretical minimum for the formation of a black hole; creates cosmic winds clocked at 20 million miles (32 million km) per hour, nearly ten times faster than has ever been observed from a stellar black hole

SOURCE NOTES

5 Kip S. Thorne, *Black Holes and Time Warps: Einstein's Outrageous Legacy* (New York: W. W. Norton, 1994), 136.

6 Carl Zimmer, "In Science, It's Never 'Just a Theory,'" *New York Times*, April 8, 2016, http://www.nytimes.com/2016/04/09 /science/in-science-its-never-just-a-theory.html?_r=1.

12 Caleb Scharf, *Gravity's Engines: How Bubble-Blowing Black Holes Rule Galaxies, Stars, and Life in the Cosmos* (New York: Scientific American/Farrar, Straus and Giroux, 2012), 15.

12 Sylvia Berryman, "Democritus," *Stanford Encyclopedia of Philosophy* (Winter 2016), https://plato.stanford.edu/archives /win2016/entries/democritus/.

14 Cian O'Luanaigh, "Fifty Years of Quarks," CERN, last modified April 10, 2014, https://home.cern/about/updates/2014/01/fifty -years-quarks.

17 Thorne, *Black Holes*, 97.

20 Jeffrey Bennett, *What Is Relativity? An Intuitive Introduction to Einstein's Ideas, and Why They Matter* (New York: Columbia University Press, 2014), 118.

20 Marcia Bartusiak, *Black Hole: How an Idea Abandoned by Newtonians, Hated by Einstein, and Gambled on by Hawking Became Loved,* (New Haven CT, Yale University Press, 2015), 30.

23 C. Renée James, *Science Unshackled: How Obscure, Abstract, Seemingly Useless Scientific Research Turned Out to Be the Basis for Modern Life* (Baltimore: Johns Hopkins University Press, 2014), 96.

23 John Archibald Wheeler, *Geons, Black Holes, and Quantum Foam: A Life in Physics* (New York: W. W. Norton, 2010) 297.

23 Ibid.

26 Carl Sagan, *Carl Sagan's Cosmic Connection: An Extraterrestrial Perspective* (Cambridge: Cambridge University Press, 2000), 190.

29 "Faces of Science: Tom Vestrand," Los Alamos National Laboratory, March 4, 2015, http://www.lanl.gov/science -innovation/features/faces-of-science/tom-vestrand.php.

32 Vestrand, personal communication with author, May 18, 2016.

33 "Vestrand," Los Alamos National Laboratory.

33 Vestrand, personal communication.

35 "Monster of the Milky Way," chap. 5. *Nova* video, *PBS*, http:// www.pbs.org/wgbh/nova/blackhole/program.html.

38 Andrea Ghez, "The Hunt for a Supermassive Black Hole," TEDGlobal 2009 video, 5:10, July 2009, https://www.ted .com/talks/andrea_ghez_the_hunt_for_a_supermassive_black_ hole?language=en.

40 Ibid., 9:01.

41 Andrea Ghez, personal communication, May 9, 2016.

41 Ibid.

46 Stuart Wolpert, "UCLA Astronomers Solve Puzzle about Bizarre Object at the Center of Our Galaxy," news release, UCLA, November 3, 2014, http://newsroom.ucla.edu/releases/ucla -astronomers-solve-puzzle-about-bizarre-object-at-the-center-of -our-galaxy.

45 Ghez, personal communication.

48 Neil deGrasse Tyson, *Death by Black Hole: And Other Cosmic Quandaries* (New York: W. W. Norton, 2007), 285.

50 Leonard Susskind, *The Black Hole War: My Battle with Stephen Hawking to Make the World Safe for Quantum Mechanics* (New York: Little, Brown, 2008), 83.

51 Walter Isaacson, *Einstein: His Life and Universe* (New York: Simon & Schuster, 2008), 448—53.

53 Stephen W. Hawking, Malcolm J. Perry, and Andrew Strominger, "Soft Hair on Black Holes," *Physical Review Letters* 116, no. 23 (June 6, 2016), http://journals.aps.org/prl/abstract/10.1103 /PhysRevLett.116.231301.

53 Dennis Overbye, "No Escape from Black Holes? Stephen Hawking Points to a Possible Exit," *New York Times*, June 16, 2016, http://www.nytimes.com/2016/06/07/science/stephen-hawking -black-holes.html?_r=0.

56 Megan Fellman, "Northwestern Astrophysicists Part of Historic Discovery," news release, Northwestern University, February 11, 2016, http://www.northwestern.edu/newscenter /stories/2016/02/astrophysicists-part-of-historic-discovery.html.

57 "LIGO Detects Gravitational Waves—Announcement at Press Conference (Part 1)," YouTube video, 3:58—4:35, posted by the National Science Foundation, February 11, 2016, https://www .youtube.com/watch?v=aEPIwEJmZyE.

57 Barack Obama (@POTUS), "Einstein was right! Congrats to @NSF and @LIGO on detecting gravitational waves—a huge breakthrough in how we understand the universe," February 11, 2016, 3:43 p.m., https://twitter.com/potus44/status/69792891 3457188864?lang=en.

66 Gabriela González, "How Gravitational Waves Were Converted into Audio 'Chirps,'" American Astronomical Society Press Conference video, June 15, 2016, available online at space.com, http://www.space.com/33180-how-gravitational -waves-were-converted-into-audio-chirps-video.html.

67 Vicky Kalogera, personal communication with author, July 19, 2016.

58 Kalogera, personal communication.

58 Ibid.

78—79 Katie Bouman, personal communication with author, July 29, 2016.

80 Ibid.

80 Ibid.

80 Ibid.

81 Ibid.

81 Ibid.

82 Ibid.

82 Ibid.

88 Eric Schlegel, personal communication with author, July 27, 2016.

88 Ibid.

89 Ibid.

89 Ibid.

89 Merrit Kennedy, "Scientists Spot 'Burping' Black Hole in Nearby Galaxy," *NPR*, January 6, 2016, http://www.npr.org/sections/thetwo-way/2016/01/06/462138463/scientists-spot-burping-black-hole-in-nearby-galaxy.

90 Eric Schlegel, "Eric Schlegel, Ph.D.,—UTSA Physics and Astronomy," YouTube video, 2:05, posted by UTSA Video Production Group on October 22, 2014, https://www.youtube.com/watch?v=895NdFwbKgk.

91 Editors of *Sky and Telescope*, "Q&A: Understanding the Fermi Bubbles," *Sky and Telescope*, February 6, 2015, http://www.skyandtelescope.com/astronomy-resources/understanding-fermi-bubbles/.

92 John Matson, "Hidden in Plain Sight: Researchers Find Galaxy-Scale Bubbles Extending from the Milky Way," *Scientific American*, November 15, 2010, http://www.scientificamerican.com/article/fermi-bubbles/.

96 "Strange but True: Black Holes Sing," *Scientific American*, October 18, 2007, http://www.scientificamerican.com/article/strange-but-true-black-holes-sing/.

97 Carl Sagan, *Cosmos* (New York: Ballantine Books, 2013), 244.

98 "The Q&A: Caleb Scharf, Engines of Creation," *Babbage* (blog), *Economist*, April 18, 2012, http://www.economist.com/blogs/babbage/2012/08/qa-caleb-scharf.

98 John Michell, "On the Means of Discovering the Distance, Magnitude, &c. of the Fixed Stars, in Consequence of the Diminution of the Velocity of Their Light, in Case Such a Diminution Should Be Found to Take Place in Any of Them, and Such Other Data Should Be Procured from Observations, as Would be Farther Necessary for That Purpose," *Philosophical Translations Royal Society of London* 1784, no. 74: 35–57, http://rstl.royalsocietypublishing.org/content/74/35.

GLOSSARY

absolute: something that is the same as measured in each and every frame of reference. Newton thought that space and time were absolute. Einstein said that space and time vary with an observer's motion.

astronomer: a scientist who uses telescopes to observe cosmic objects or events

astrophysicist: a physicist who specializes in studying cosmic objects and events

atom: a building block of matter. Atoms are made of protons, neutrons, and electrons.

big bang: the scientific theory that says that all space, time, matter, and energy in our universe originated from the violent explosion of a single point of extremely high density and temperature about 13.8 billion years ago

binary system: two objects in orbit around each other. They may be two stars or two black holes or a star and a black hole.

black hole: an object whose mass is concentrated in a point of almost infinite density, with such powerful gravity that nothing can escape from it. Black holes seem to be at the center of galaxies and are the place where stars collapse and are born.

blueshift: a shift of electromagnetic waves from longer (red) to shorter wavelengths on the blue end of the visible electromagnetic spectrum, indicating that an object is moving away from the observer

corpuscle: the word scientists in the seventeenth and eighteenth centuries used for light particles

cosmic ray: a high energy particle that bombards Earth from space

dark energy: a theoretical force that counteracts gravity. Scientists believe it is the best explanation for the accelerating rate of the expansion of the universe. Dark energy makes up about 68 percent of all cosmic matter.

dark matter: matter that exists in the universe but that humans cannot detect because it emits no radiation that we can observe. Scientists believe it exists because it exerts gravitational forces that affect astronomical objects. Dark matter makes up about 27 percent of all cosmic matter.

Doppler shift: the shift of a wave to a higher frequency (shorter wavelength) when the source is moving toward the observer and to a lower frequency (longer wavelength) when the source is moving away from the observer

electromagnetic (EM) radiation: energy that takes the form of electric and magnetic waves, as well as a stream of photons, traveling at the speed of light in a vacuum

electromagnetic spectrum: the entire range of all the various kinds of electromagnetic radiation, including (from short to long wavelengths): gamma rays, X-rays, ultraviolet, optical (visible light), infrared, microwave, and radio waves. The shorter the wavelength, the higher the frequency and energy. The longer the wavelength, the lower the frequency and energy.

electron: a negatively charged elementary particle that exists in a cloud surrounding the outer regions of atoms

elliptical: oval-shaped, like an ellipse

escape velocity: the minimum speed necessary for something to escape the gravitational pull of a celestial body. A rocket launched from Earth must accelerate to about 25,000 miles (40,234 km) to escape Earth's gravitational pull and travel to another planet. Scientists calculate the escape velocity from a black hole to be greater than the speed of light, which is impossible. This means that nothing can escape a black hole.

ether: a historical term scientists used to talk about the medium or material they thought filled the universe. In the nineteenth century, scientists thought ether was the medium through which light could travel.

event horizon: a black hole's point of no return. Any light or matter that crosses beyond the event horizon cannot cross back. Although it is not a physical boundary, the event horizon marks the exterior "surface" of a black hole.

field: something that is distributed continuously and smoothly in space, such as an electric field or magnetic field

frequency: the rate at which a wave oscillates, or vibrates. Frequency refers to the number of cycles of oscillations per second. These oscillations are measured from the crest (or peak) of one wave to the crest of the next.

galaxy: a collection of one billion to one trillion stars that all orbit around a common center

gamma rays: electromagnetic waves with extremely short wavelengths and high frequencies

general relativity: Albert Einstein's theory, published in 1915, in which he described gravity as a curvature of both space and time (space-time)

gravity: a fundamental force that causes two massive objects to be attracted toward each other

infrared radiation: electromagnetic waves with a wavelength a little longer than visible light. We can't see infrared radiation with our eyes, but we can feel and measure it as heat.

interferometry: the process in which two or more waves interfere with each other. Scientists use interferometry to make very small measurements and to measure tiny distances between objects.

jet: a beam of gas that carries energy outward from a black hole

light-year: the distance that light travels in one year, at the rate of 664 million miles (1.1 billion km) per hour. One light-year is equivalent to 5.9 trillion miles (9.5 trillion km).

mass: a measure of the amount of matter in an object. Mass is always a fixed quantity for any given object and is not the same as weight. Scientists measure mass in kilograms.

matter: anything that has mass

microwave: electromagnetic radiation with a wavelength a little shorter than radio waves

Milky Way: the spiral galaxy in which we live. It is so named because it appears as a faint whitish band stretching across the night sky.

molecule: a group of two or more atoms that are held together by chemical bonds. Molecules do not have an electrical charge.

neutrino: a fundamental particle produced in massive numbers by nuclear reactions in stars. They are very difficult to detect because they interact very weakly with matter. All the same, scientists have found a variety of sophisticated technologies to detect them.

neutron: an electrically neutral subatomic particle. Together with protons, neutrons make up the nucleus of an atom.

neutron star: the compressed core of an exploded star composed almost entirely of neutrons. They have strong gravitational fields. Some emit pulses of energy along their axes and are known as pulsars.

nuclear fusion: the process in which two atomic nuclei merge to form a larger nucleus. The process creates a great deal of energy and is the force scientists use to make hydrogen bombs. In the sun and most stars, hydrogen nuclei fuse together to form helium.

nucleus: in physics, the dense core of an atom

particle: in physics, a particle is a tiny bundle of mass or energy. Particles are the building blocks of matter, including protons, neutrons, and electrons, as well as photons, quarks, and neutrinos.

photon: a particle of light, a packet of electromagnetic radiation

planet: a spherical ball that orbits a star. Planets can be made of rock, gas, or both. Earth, for example, is a rocky planet, while Jupiter is a gas planet.

primordial black hole: a black hole, typically less massive than a solar black hole, thought to have formed shortly after the big bang

proton: a positively charged subatomic particle. Together with neutrons, protons make up the nucleus of an atom.

quantum mechanics: the laws of physics that govern the realm of the very small (atoms and subatomic particles). These laws are also known as quantum theory.

radiation: energy emitted in the form of waves or particles

radio waves: electromagnetic waves of a very low frequency (long wavelength). Radio waves are used to receive and transmit signals between two objects, and astronomers also used naturally occurring radio waves to study certain objects in space.

redshift: a shift of electromagnetic waves from shorter (blue) to longer wavelengths on the red end of the visible EM spectrum, indicating that an object is moving away from the observer

relative: an observation that depends on the observer's reference frame

rotation: the spin of a body about its axis, or the imaginary line through its center

shock: unusually high pressures that in the universe are produced by the movement of exploding gas

singularity: a one-dimensional point that contains a huge mass in an infinitely small space. In this point, space-time curves infinitely and the laws of physics as we understand them no longer work.

space-time: the mathematical model that combines the three dimensions of space with a fourth dimension, time. A point in space-time is defined by its three space coordinates and its time coordinate. In the general theory of relativity, the curvature of space-time is responsible for the phenomenon we know as gravity.

special relativity: Albert Einstein's theory, published in 1905, to explain the fundamentals of space, time, and motion, in the absence of gravity. The theory is based on the principle that the laws of physics, including the speed of light, are the same for all non-accelerating observers. It leads to the prediction that objects moving at nearly the speed of light contract and that their time slows down.

speed of light: 186,000 miles (299,338 km) per second, the speed at which electromagnetic radiation, or light, travels through a vacuum

star: a giant ball of hot gas held together by its own gravity that generates nuclear energy in its core through nuclear fusion. The energy released in that reaction is emitted as visible light and other forms of electromagnetic radiation.

stellar black hole: a black hole formed by the gravitational collapse of a massive star

supernova: a gigantic explosion of a dying star; the energy released when a star's inner core explodes and then powers the explosion of a star's outer layers

tidal force: the gravitational pull on planetary objects from nearby planets and moons. For example, the movement of Earth's oceans is impacted by our moon. In a black hole, extreme tidal forces cause the vertical stretching and horizontal compression of objects.

ultraviolet light: electromagnetic radiation whose wavelength is a little shorter than the light on the violet end of the spectrum of visible light

vacuum: a region from which all particles, fields, and energy have been removed or do not exist

wavelength: the distance between the two crests, or peaks, of a wave

white dwarf star: a small white star, about the diameter of Earth, that is the remnant of a star that has exhausted all of its nuclear fuel and is cooling off. The sun will one day become a white dwarf star.

wormhole: a hypothetical tunnel, or connection, that may link two widely separated regions of space-time. Although there is no observational evidence for wormholes, the mathematics of the general theory of relativity predict that they are theoretically possible.

X-rays: electromagnetic waves with a wavelength between that of ultraviolet radiation on the red end of the electromagnetic spectrum and gamma rays on the blue end of the spectrum

Bennett, Jeffrey. *What Is Relativity? An Intuitive Introduction to Einstein's Ideas, and Why They Matter*. New York: Columbia University Press, 2014.

deGrasse Tyson, Neil. *Death by Black Hole: And Other Cosmic Quandaries*. New York: W. W. Norton, 2007.

———. *Welcome to the Universe: An Astrophysical Tour*. Princeton, NJ: Princeton University Press, 2016.

Hawking, Stephen. *A Brief History of Time: From the Big Bang to Black Holes*. New York: Bantam Books, 1998.

Levin, Janna. *Black Hole Blues and Other Songs from Outer Space*. New York: Alfred A. Knopf, 2016.

Roach, Mary. *Packing for Mars: The Curious Science of Life in the Void*. New York: W. W. Norton, 2011.

Scharf, Caleb. *Gravity's Engines: How Bubble-Blowing Black Holes Rule Galaxies, Stars, and Life in the Cosmos*. New York: Scientific American/Farrar, Straus and Giroux, 2012.

Strathern, Paul. *The Big Idea: Einstein and Relativity*. New York: Anchor Books, 1997.

Thorne, Kip. *Black Holes and Time Warps: Einstein's Outrageous Legacy*. New York: W. W. Norton, 1994.

———. *The Science of Interstellar*. New York: W. W. Norton, 2014.

BOOKS

Grant, John. Eureka!: *50 Scientists Who Shaped Human History*. San Francisco: Zest Books, 2016.

Kruesi, Liz. *Astronomy*. Minneapolis: Abdo Publishing, 2016.

Moore, Patrick. *Exploring the Mysteries of Astronomy*. New York: Rosen Publishing, 2017.

FILMS AND DOCUMENTARIES

Ghez, Andrea. "The Hunt for a Supermassive Black Hole." TEDGlobal 2009, 16:26. July 2009. https://www.ted.com/talks/andrea_ghez_the_hunt_for_a_supermassive_black_hole?language=en. With new data from the Keck telescopes, Ghez shows how state-of-the-art adaptive optics are helping astronomers understand our universe's most mysterious objects: black holes.

Green, Hank. "What Stephen Hawking Really Said about Black Holes," 4:27. Posted by "SciShow," February 14, 2014. https://www.youtube.com/watch?v=L8GCR88T3fE.
In this episode of the popular SciShow web series, Hank Green explains what Stephen Hawking meant when he said there are no black holes.

"Inside Einstein's Mind." *Nova*, 53:07. First broadcast on PBS on November 25, 2015. http://www.pbs.org/video/2365615918/.
In celebration of the one-hundredth anniversary of the publication of Einstein's general theory of relativity, *Nova* tells the inside story of his masterpiece.

"Neil deGrasse Tyson—Death by Black Hole." YouTube video, 31:14. Posted by "jesamus charrist," September 12, 2016. https://www.youtube.com/watch?v=C85roOeyfek.
Astrophysicist Neil deGrasse Tyson explains the hypothetical experience of death by falling into a black hole.

WEBSITES

Chandra X-ray Observatory
http://chandra.harvard.edu/
The Chandra website is a rich source of information about discoveries made using the Chandra telescope as well as more general information about X-ray astronomy, black holes, and other astronomical objects.

Einstein Online

http://www.einstein-online.info/

This website provides information about Einstein's theories of relativity and the coolest applications, from the smallest particles to black holes and cosmology. It contains historical information as well as recent discoveries related to Einstein's theories.

Event Horizon Telescope

http://www.eventhorizontelescope.org/

The key science objectives of the Event Horizon Telescope, technical and science requirements, the primary observing targets (including Sagittarius A*), and key science results are featured at this site.

Fermi Gamma-ray Space Telescope

http://fermi.gsfc.nasa.gov/

The gamma ray space telescope's mission to observe the cosmos using the highest-energy form of light, providing a window into black hole jets, supernova remnants, and more are available at this site. The site includes links to related topics, such as dark energy and dark matter, active galactic nuclei, and other research at NASA.

"Imagine the Universe!"

http://imagine.gsfc.nasa.gov/home.html

Intended for students aged fourteen and older, this site includes pages on black holes and other astronomical objects as well as games, scientist profiles, new discoveries, and more.

"Inside Black Holes"

http://jila.colorado.edu/~ajsh/insidebh/

This website takes the viewer inside black holes using computer-generated visualizations.

Keck Observatory

http://www.keckobservatory.org/

This is the official website of the Keck Observatory, which has the world's largest and most scientifically productive optical and infrared telescopes. The site includes recent news about scientific discoveries, photos, and videos.

LIGO Scientific Collaboration

http://www.ligo.org/

The official website of the LIGO collaboration has up-to-date news and discoveries, along with good explanations of the science behind the project. Of special interest is the page "Comparing 'Chirps' from Black Holes," where the best-fit models of LIGO's gravitational wave signals are converted into sounds.

astrophysics, 63, 96
Atacama Large Millimeter/
    submillimeter Array (ALMA),
    77
atomic clock, 68, 78

big bang theory, 35, 61, 97
binary black holes, 59, 63
binary stars, 46, 63
    G2, 44, 46
black holes, 5, 28–29
    entanglement, 52
    event horizon, 22, 31, 46–48,
        52–53, 73–76, 83
    galaxies, 5, 34–35, 38,
        73–74, 81, 87–89, 92,
        96–97
    gravitational waves, 7, 55, 57,
        59, 62
    history of black hole theories,
        5, 7, 12, 22–23, 25–26
    infographics, 46, 56
    mass, 5, 12, 23, 34, 38, 59,
        92–93
    spaghettification, 48
    supermassive black holes,
        34–35, 61–62, 74, 87, 92
Bohr, Niels, 50–51
Bouman, Katie, 78–82

Continuous High-resolution
    Image Reconstruction using
    Patch priors (CHIRP), 79
corpuscles, 12
cosmic explosions, 29
    gamma ray bursts, 29, 33
Cygnus X-1, 24–25

dark energy, 60–61
    theory of expanding universe,
        60
dark matter, 60–61, 70, 91
    detection in space, 60
    and primordial black holes, 61

Doppler shift, 42
    redshift, 60

Eddington, Arthur, 19–20
Einstein, Albert, 7, 14–17,
    20–21, 31, 51
    and black holes, 5
    general theory of relativity, 5,
        7, 16–17
    special theory of relativity, 14
Einstein-Rosen bridge, 31
electromagnetic spectrum,
    10–11, 42–43, 60
    infographic, 10
electromagnetic radiation, 12,
    29, 56
escape velocity, 9, 22
event horizon, 22, 31, 52–53,
    73–76, 83
Event Horizon Telescope (EHT),
    75–80, 82–83
    Continuous High-resolution
        Image Reconstruction using
        Patch priors (CHIRP), 79
Exposition du système du monde
    (Explanation of the System
    of the World) (Laplace), 12

Fabian, Andrew, 94
Fermi Gamma-ray Space
    Telescope, 91–92
    Fermi Bubbles, 91–93
Finkbeiner, Douglas, 91–92
Flamm, Ludwig, 30–31
    white holes, 31
frame of reference, 15–16

galactic nuclei, 38
galaxies, 4–5, 34–35, 38, 40,
    42, 60, 81, 87–88, 92,
    96–97
    M87, 74, 83, 96
    Milky Way, 37–40, 73–75,
        89, 91–93, 98

Perseus, 93–96
  spiral, 86, 89
  Whirlpool, 86, 88
gamma rays, 11, 29, 43, 91
  Fermi Bubbles, 91–93
  gamma ray bursts, 29, 32–33
  GRB 130427A, 32
Ghez, Andrea, 37–41, 44–46
  adaptive optics, 40
Global Positioning System (GPS),
  68–69
  satellites, 68–69
gravitational waves, 7, 54–59,
  62–67, 70–71, 73
gravity, 6–9, 16–18, 21–22,
  28, 46–48, 57, 60–61, 95
G2, 44, 46
  Keck Observatory, 36–37, 40
  Sagittarius A*, 44
  SO-2, 40

Hawking, Stephen, 49, 52–53
  Hawking radiation, 49, 52
  quantum theory, 52–53
  "Soft Hair on Black Holes," 53

infographics, 19, 35, 43, 46,
  56, 61, 65, 78
interferometry, 79
Interstellar, 30, 47

Kalogera, Vicky, 55–58, 63, 67,
  70

Laplace, Pierre-Simon, 12, 22
  Exposition du système du monde
    (Explanation of the System
    of the World), 12
Laser Interferometer
  Gravitational-Wave
  Observatory (LIGO), 55–59,
  61–70
  binary black hole collisions, 59,
    62–63, 70

gravitational waves, 63–67,
  70
  sound waves, 66–67

mass, 5, 8–9, 12, 17–18,
  22–23, 26–27, 38–39, 59
matter, 12–13, 17–18, 21, 31,
  50, 89, 97
  dark energy, 60–61
  dark matter, 70, 91
  ordinary matter, 60
Maxwell, James Clerk, 12
  electromagnetic radiation, 12
M87 black hole, 74, 83, 96
Michell, John, 9, 12, 98–99
  dark stars, 9, 22, 98
Milky Way galaxy, 37–40,
  73–75, 89, 91–93, 98

neutron stars, 25, 27, 71
Newton, Isaac, 6–9, 14, 16, 20
  laws of motion, 7–8
  Philosophiæ Naturalis
    Principia Mathematica
    (Mathematical Principals of
    Natural Philosophy), 7–8
nuclear fusion, 22–23, 26, 41

Oppenheimer, J. Robert, 22
optical telescopes, 25
  Hubble Space Telescope, 39,
    70, 87
  Keck telescopes, 36–37, 40
  Kitt Peak National Observa-
    tory, 87
  RAPid Telescopes for Optical
    Response (RAPTOR),
    32–33

Perseus black hole, 93–96
  sound waves, 94
Philosophiæ Naturalis
  Principia Mathematica
  (Mathematical Principals

of Natural Philosophy)
(Newton), 7—8
profiles
Katie Bouman, 80—81
Andrea Ghez, 45
Vicky Kalogera, 58
Eric Schlegel, 90
Tom Vestrand, 33

quantum entanglement, 51—52
quantum mechanics, 49—50, 52
wave-particle duality, 50
quantum theory, 50—51

radio astronomy, 77
radio waves, 79, 94
radio telescopes, 75, 79
Atacama Large Millimeter/
submillimeter Array (ALMA),
77
Event Horizon Telescope (EHT),
75—80, 82—83
Shanghai Astronomical
Observatory, 75
Very Long Baseline Array
(VLBA), 76
red giant, 26
redshift, 43, 60
relativity
general theory of relativity,
5, 7, 16—17, 21, 49, 52,
56—58, 69, 83
special theory of relativity, 14,
68

Sagan, Carl, 30, 97
Sagittarius A*, 38, 40—41, 44,
61, 73—76, 78—79, 81—83,
89, 92
Scharf, Caleb, 98
Schlegel, Eric, 86—90
Schwarzschild, Karl, 21—22
Schwarzschild metric, 22
Schwarzschild radius, 22
Shen, Zhiqiang, 75
first image of a black hole,

75—76
singularity, 22, 46, 49
"Soft Hair on Black Holes,"
(Hawking, Perry, and
Strominger) 53
space-time, 14, 17—18, 20—22,
30, 48, 57, 83
speed of light, 64, 83, 96
stars, 25—27, 40, 42—43, 46,
88—89
death of, 26, 29, 92
formation of, 26, 41, 63, 89,
92
subatomic particles, 23, 50
supernova explosions, 63, 86, 97

telescopes
optical telescopes, 25
radio telescopes, 75, 79
space-based X-ray telescopes,
24, 29
Tyson, Neil deGrasse, 34—35

Uhuru, 24—25

Very Long Baseline Array (VLBA),
76
first image of a black hole, 76
Vestrand, Tom, 29, 32—33

Wheeler, John Archibald, 23
white dwarf star, 26—27, 85
wormhole, 30—31

X-ray astronomy, 94
X-ray telescopes, 24—25, 29
Chandra Observatory, 39, 70,
84—87, 94—95

PHOTO ACKNOWLEDGMENTS

The images in this book are used with the permission of: © iStockphoto.com/maciek905 (design element throughout); X-ray: NASA/CXC/Caltech/P.Ogle et al.; Optical: NASA/ STScI; IR: NASA/JPL-Caltech; Radio: NSF/NRAO/VLA, p. 4; © SSPL/Science Museum/Getty Images, p. 8; NASA, pp.10, 62, 69, 81, 84, 95, © Universal History Archive/UIG/Getty Images, p. 15;© ESA—C.Carreau, p. 18; © Laura Westlund/ Independent Picture Service, pp. 19, 35, 43, 46, 65, 78; © AIP Emilio Segre Visual Archives, p. 21; © SSPL/Getty Images, p. 24; ktsdesign/Shutterstock.com, p. 29; NASA/ Swift/Stefan Immler, p. 31; Courtesy of the Los Alamos National Laboratory Archives, p. 33;© Jesse Dittmar/Redux, p. 34; Richard Wainscoat/Alamy Stock Photo, p. 36; X-ray: NASA/UMass/D.Wang et al., IR: NASA/STScI, p. 39; ESO/ MPE/Marc Schartmann, p. 44; © ANNIE TRITT/The New York Times/Redux, p. 45; © 2013 Karwai Tang/Getty Images, p. 49; © Paul Ehrenfest (1880-1933)/Wikimedia Commons (public domain), p. 51; LIGO/Axel Mellinger, p. 54; Caltech/MIT/LIGO Lab, p. 56; Ann Feild (STScI)/NASA, p. 61; NASA, ESA, CFHT, CXO, M.J. Jee (University of California, Davis), and A. Mahdavi (San Francisco State University), p. 70; NASA/JPL-Caltech, p. 72; NASA/CXC/W. Forman et al., p. 74; © Meridith Kohut/The New York Time/Redux, p. 76; NASA/CXC/SAO, pp. 87, 100, 102 (bottom); NASA/ESA, p. 90; NASA/Goddard Space Flight Center, p. 93; NASA, ESA, Digitized Sky Survey 2, p. 101.

Front cover: © iStockphoto.com/vchal.

Sara Latta is the author of more than twenty nonfiction and science books for children and young adults. Recent titles include *Scared Stiff: Everything You Need to Know about 50 Famous Phobias* and *Smash! Exploring the Mysteries of the Universe with the Large Hadron Collider*.

A would-be scientist, she earned her master's degree in immunology before deciding that she'd rather write about science instead. A midwestern sunflower transplanted to New York City, she enjoys exploring the city, playing with her dog, and learning to make pottery. For more information, check out her website at http://www.saralatta.com.